More Praise for *Out of Poverty*

"Drawing on his own firsthand experiences and in-person observations, Paul Polak's book goes straight to the heart of the matter and offers how-to advice on wiping out global poverty, one family and one person at a time. Half the people on Earth live on less than four dollars a day—the rest of us should read this book."

> —David M. Kelley, Founder and Chairman, IDEO, and Donald W. Whittier Professor in Mechanical Engineering, Stanford University

"As the US Army becomes more heavily involved in stability and support operations around the world, Dr. Polak's radical and direct approach to combating global poverty is proving to be practical, effective, and deeply influential to policy makers at all levels."

> —Colonel Martin Leppert

"With personal anecdotes and field experiences, Paul Polak shares the philosophies that have made IDE one of the most successful organizations in providing life-changing technologies to people in the developing world. Paul's *joie de vivre*, his commitment to eliminating poverty, and his pragmatic irreverence are all captured in his book."

> —Amy Smith, Senior Lecturer, Department of Mechanical Engineering, MIT

"Paul Polak offers a personal, radical, and profoundly sensible prescription for alleviating global poverty. His engaging style of storytelling is not only persuasive but entertaining. Read *Out of Poverty*—it will change the way you look at the world."

> —Sandra Postel, Director, Global Water Policy Project, and author of *Pillar of Sand: Can the Irrigation Miracle Last?*

"Paul Polak provides a unique, practical, and entrepreneurial blueprint to enable and empower the rural poor to lift themselves out of poverty. His innovative and curious mind and his courage in challenging conventional thinking offer proven solutions that unleash the capacity of the poor to create income—giving them a hand up, not a handout."

> —Philip R Berber, Chairman, A Glimmer of Hope Foundation

"*Out of Poverty* is very exciting. It matches a lot of my own thoughts about solving things. When you alleviate something but don't fix the cause, it comes back. Paul Polak's approach confronts the root causes."

—Steve Wozniak, inventor of the Apple computer and cofounder, Apple Computer

"Viewing the poor as passive recipients of assistance has wasted billions of dollars. Top-down, bailout subsidy programs don't work. As Paul explains, we need to partner with the developing world and provide tools and technologies to give them an opportunity to help themselves."

—Shrikrishna Upadhyay, Founder, SAPPROS, Nepal

"Paul Polak listens to people few of us ever hear from—the world's poor 'one-acre farmers'—and comes up with simple, practical solutions for helping them better their lives. His work is profoundly inspiring."

—Lori Pottinger, Editor, *World Rivers Review* and Africa Campaigns, International Rivers

"Paul Polak delivers a refreshing dose of common sense to the question of how best to help the world's poorest citizens, the common sense born of a lifetime of hands-on experience. It serves as a how-to manual for Stanford's course on Design for Extreme Affordability."

—James M. Patell, Herbert Hoover Professor of Public and Private Management, Graduate School of Business, Stanford University

"Paul Polak is passionate about the alleviation of poverty. This book presents numerous case studies demonstrating that effective programs to raise the incomes of poor people must start with an effort to understand and involve poor people in the environments in which they find themselves."

—Vernon W. Ruttan, Regents' Professor Emeritus, Departments of Economics and Applied Economics, University of Minnesota

"Paul's approach to solving our world's greatest ailment is one of simplicity in design and humanity in spirit. His powerful recipe for change is clear, precise, and doable. And we desperately need to do it right now."

—John Maeda, President, Rhode Island School of Design, and author of *The Laws of Simplicity*

"*Out of Poverty* is an 'unputdownable' record of Polak's success with tiny-scale farmers, embedded with workable rules for designing, scaling up, and distributing affordable innovations to the poor. It makes a clear declaration: Poverty can be ended if business, government, and development agencies learn these lessons."
    —**Michael Lipton, Research Professor, Poverty Research Unit, University of Sussex**

"Paul Polak's book is not merely an incredibly inspiring personal story. It is also an engaging series of practical lessons, a field guide for practitioners that is destined to be underlined and dog-eared. This is a book for people who want to go deeper."
    —**Andrew Youn, founder, One Acre Fund**

"The only economic ideology that can move a large number of people out of poverty in a sustainable manner is the one based on entrepreneurship... Dr. Polak's book clearly defines how entrepreneurship can be implemented for smallholders in rural areas, which is critical since 80 percent of the extremely poor fall in this category... I anticipate that some of you will read this book and, just like me, decide you can follow its model to bring more hope to your part of the world."
    —**Mohsen Rezayat, PhD, President and CEO, OMID USA**

Paul's ideas have helped bring millions of people out of poverty, and, along the way, he has ignited a design revolution that offers us all a bright new way to look at the world."
    —**Michael Cronan, Cronan Design**

"Paul Polak's insights open new vistas in design discovery. *Out of Poverty* is one of the clearest descriptions of how design has a profound impact on the cycle of poverty and really changes the world."
    —**Yves Behar, President and Creative Director, fuseproject, and Chair of Industrial Design, California College of the Arts**

"Paul Polak's method works because it harnesses the power of design thinking, low-cost technology, and human enterprise to create sustainable communities of trade. Paul's remarkable work has eliminated poverty and restored dignity to millions of families."
    —**Ann Willoughby, President and Creative Director, Willoughby Design**

Out of Poverty

WHAT WORKS WHEN TRADITIONAL APPROACHES FAIL

Paul Polak

Berrett–Koehler Publishers, Inc.
San Francisco
a BK Currents book

Berrett-Koehler Publishers, Inc.
235 Montgomery Street, Suite 650, San Francisco, CA 94104-2916
Tel: (415) 288-0260 Fax: (415) 362-2512 www.bkconnection.com

Ordering Information

Quantity sales. Special discounts are available on quantity purchases by corporations, associations, and others. For details, contact the "Special Sales Department" at the Berrett-Koehler address above.

Individual sales. Berrett-Koehler publications are available through most bookstores. They can also be ordered directly from Berrett-Koehler: Tel: (800) 929-2929; Fax: (802) 864-7626; www.bkconnection.com.

Orders for college textbook/course adoption use. Please contact Berrett-Koehler: Tel: (800) 929-2929; Fax: (802) 864-7626.

Orders by U.S. trade bookstores and wholesalers. Please contact Ingram Publisher Services, Tel: (800) 509-4887; Fax: (800) 838-1149; E-mail: customer.service@ingrampublisher services.com; or visit www.ingrampublisherservices.com/Ordering for details about electronic ordering.

Berrett-Koehler and the BK logo are registered trademarks of Berrett-Koehler Publishers, Inc.

Printed in the United States of America

Berrett-Koehler books are printed on long-lasting acid-free paper. When it is available, we choose paper that has been manufactured by environmentally responsible processes. These may include using trees grown in sustainable forests, incorporating recycled paper, minimizing chlorine in bleaching, or recycling the energy produced at the paper mill.

Library of Congress Cataloging-in-Publication Data

Polak, Paul.
Out of poverty : what works when traditional approaches fail / Paul Polak.
   p.   cm.
Includes bibliographical references.
ISBN 978-1-57675-449-8 (hardcover: alk. paper)
ISBN 978-1-60509-276-8 (pbk.: alk. paper)
1. Poverty. I. Title.
hc79.p6p66 2008
362.5'6—dc22   2007041387

First Edition

14 13 12 11 10 09   10 9 8 7 6 5 4 3 2 1

Photo on cover and pg 170: © Keren Su/Corbis. All other photos © Paul Polak, IDE

Book design and production management by Valerie Brewster, Scribe Typography.
Copyediting by Don Roberts. Proofreading by Don Roberts and Sarah Muirhead.
Indexing by Rachel Rice: Directions Unlimited. Cover design: Pema Studios.

✣ For my wife, Aggie, my daughters—Amy, Kathryn, and Laura—
and for small-acreage farmers like Krishna Bahadur Thapa who put
music into the words

CONTENTS

PREFACE

My fifteen-month-old grandson, Ethan, has fallen in love with a neighbor's driveway. It sits two houses down from where he lives in Sebastopol, California, and it seems to overflow with small, multicolored stones. He stops there when I take him for a walk, and then he refuses to leave. He picks up a handful of stones and inspects each one carefully. He places them one after another in my hand, watching intently, and I give them back to him one by one until his hand is full again. I don't know who has given him the job of turning every little stone over and over in his hand until he understands its very essence, but that's the job he has accepted, and he's not leaving until it's done. He plops down on his butt and cuffs the stones into a pile, looks at me, and knocks it down and giggles. He can keep this up for hours, and if I pick him up to take him home, he cries. His playful curiosity is infectious, and I think I must have inherited a lot of genes from Ethan, because I operate just as he does. I live to play and to satisfy my curiosity.

For the past twenty-five years, two questions have kept my curiosity aroused: What makes poor people poor? And what can they do about their poverty?

Because of these infernal questions, I've dozed off during hundreds of long jeep rides with good companions over dusty, potholed roads. I've had thousands of conversations with one-acre farmers with dirt on their hands. We've walked along their patches of ten-foot-high black pepper vines in the central hills of Vietnam beside jungle permanently scarred by Agent Orange. We've strolled together through their scattered quarter-acre plots in the drab brown winter plains of the Gangetic delta in Uttar Pradesh, and they have offered me more cups of steaming tea than my seventy-three-year-old kidneys can take. I love discovering new things from people nobody else ever seems to listen to, and I love talking them into trying out some of the crazy ideas that we come up with together. I have learned more from talking with these poor farmers than from any other thing I have done in my life.

This book will tell their story and describe some of the things these people have taught me. It will tell the story of Krishna Bahadur Thapa and his family, and of how they moved from barely surviving on less than a dollar a day to earning forty-eight hundred dollars a year from their two-acre farm in the hills of Nepal. I tell many stories like Bahadur's in this book, and I hope that each one of them satisfies another small bit of your curiosity about how people who are extremely poor live their lives and dream their dreams. Best of all, what I learned from these people has been put to work in straightforward strategies that millions of other poor people have used to end their poverty forever.

Each of the practical solutions to poverty I describe is obvious and direct. For example, since 800 million of the people whose families survive on less than a dollar a day earn their living from small farms, why not start by looking for ways they can make more money from farming? And since these farmers work for less than a dollar a day, why not look for ways they can take advantage of their remarkably low labor rates by growing high-value, labor-intensive cash crops and selling them at the time of year when these crops will fetch the highest prices? If it is true that common sense is not really common, and that seeing and doing the obvious are even less so, then some of the conclusions I draw from my conversations with poor people will surprise you: they certainly fly in the face of conventional theory and practice in the development field.

I hate books about poverty that make you feel guilty, as well as dry, academic ones that put you to sleep. Working to alleviate poverty is a lively, exciting field capable of generating new hope and inspiration, not feelings of gloom and doom. Learning the truth about poverty generates disruptive innovations capable of enriching the lives of rich people even more than those of poor people.

The first section of the book explains how I became curious about poverty, describes the process I learned for finding creative solutions to just about any major social problem, and challenges the three great poverty eradication myths that have inhibited doing the obvious to end poverty.

The next section, Chapters 3 to 8, describes what many small-acreage farmers have taught me, a practical approach capable of ending the poverty of some 800 million of the world's dollar-a-day people. For poor people themselves, there is little doubt that the single most important step they can take to move out of poverty is to learn how to make more money. The way to do it is through grassroots enterprises —just about all of the poor are already tough, stubborn, survival entrepreneurs—and they have to find ways to make their enterprises more profitable. For small-farm enterprises, the path to new wealth lies in growing market-centered, high-value, labor-intensive cash crops. To accomplish this, poor farmers need access to affordable irrigation, a new generation of farming methods and inputs customized to fit tiny farms, the creation of vibrant new markets that bring them the seeds and fertilizers they need, and open access to markets where small-acreage farmers can sell their products at a profit. This range of new products and services for poor customers can only be created by a revolution in current design practice, based on the ruthless pursuit of affordability. Chapter 9 describes how the principles discussed in the earlier chapters can be applied to helping poor people living in urban slums and on the sidewalks of cities in developing countries.

In the wrap-up section, Chapter 10 describes the central role poverty plays in most of the problems facing planet Earth; Chapter 11 describes what donors, governments, universities, research institutions, and the rest of us can do to end poverty; and Chapter 12 tells how Bahadur and his family finally moved out of poverty.

My hope is that you will come away from reading this book energized and inspired. There is much to be done.

Paul Polak talks with Deu Bahadur Thapa and Bhimsen Gurung in Ekle Phant village, Nepal.

Learning to Do the Simple and Obvious

I WAS TWELVE YEARS OLD WHEN I LEARNED I COULD MAKE FIVE cents a quart picking strawberries. So when strawberry-picking season rolled around in mid-June 1945, my friends and I got pretty good at it. Before the season was over, I picked two hundred quarts in one day and came home with ten dollars in my pocket. This got me to thinking.

"If I can make ten bucks a day picking strawberries," I said, "just imagine what the owner of the field is making." I decided then and there to go into the strawberry business.

So at the age of fifteen, I convinced two local farmers to be my partners. Morley Leatherdale had a job in town and raised trotting horses in his spare time. He had a nice, rolling, loamy three acres behind his house that he was willing to contribute to the strawberry business. Ed Cummins had inherited one-hundred-and-sixty acres of fine farmland from his father, along with a large Victorian red brick house that looked like a castle to me. He contributed a beautiful four-acre piece of sandy, fertile soil at the back of his farm.

The first step was putting a thick layer of manure on both fields. Ed had a barn with twenty milk cows; his cup of manure was running over. One spring morning, Ed and I hitched his team of horses to the manure spreader and started throwing manure into it with pitchforks. Ed spit on his hands and pitched forkful after forkful at a slow but steady pace. He was close to sixty and I was in very good shape, so I knew this would be a good opportunity to show him up.

"This will be a breeze," I thought, as I pitched manure at a torrid pace. I outstripped Ed easily for half an hour, but in the second half hour he seemed to be catching up. By the end of two hours, the spreader full, Ed had me beat by a mile. Worse still, he had hardly broken a sweat while I was sweating like a pig, ready to lie down and die.

When the loader was full, we ran it out to the field. Ed pulled on a long, rusty, red gear handle that activated the chain-and-ratchet mechanism connected to the rear axle, gradually feeding the manure into a rapidly rotating horizontal column of spikes at the back. Steam rose from the horses' backs in the early morning sun, and clods of cow manure flew wildly over the field. We covered the wheat-stubble surface of that field with more loads than I can remember. By the end of the day, I was exhausted. The next morning we did it all over again. Ed then plowed the wheat stubble and manure under, and leveled the field with a harrow so it was ready for the planter.

Somebody loaned us a double-row horse-drawn planter—I don't think you can find one anywhere now except in a museum. It had a tiny plow in front which opened up a six-inch-deep furrow, and two spring-based round metal seats at the back where Morley and I perched our bums precariously close to the earth as the contraption dragged along. With my right hand, I picked up a seedling from the flat in front of me and backhanded it down into the furrow. As if my mirror image, Morley did the same from the right seat. We alternated all day like two players in a never-ending, slow tennis match. As soon as we placed a plant in the furrow, the planter gave it a squirt of water from an overhead tank, then two rollers trailing along behind closed the furrow. It took us a day and a half to plant seven-and-a-half acres.

My biggest challenge after planting was to get rid of all the ragweed, pigweed, and clumps of grass that appeared out of nowhere to compete with my strawberry plants. My main accomplice in this genocidal attack on all weeds was an old horse named Dick, who had a bad gas problem and who pulled a six-tined cultivator. I grew to love the pungent smell of horse sweat mixed with the heated leather of Dick's harness. The trick for me was to weave the cultivator in and out between the plants without uprooting them. This cut down on the hoeing time.

Cultivating turned out to be a much easier job than hoeing. I could cover a lot of ground with a fast slicing motion that just missed the strawberry plants. But hoeing a four-acre strawberry field took several days, and by the time I reached the end of the last row, it was time to start again. I learned then what legions of farmers have always known: the everyday work of farming is excruciatingly boring.

At the end of that first year, the strawberry fields looked good. But unlike previous years when I had cash in my pocket from picking, I was seriously in the hole. Maybe being an owner didn't bring as much of a bonanza as I thought it would.

When harvesttime came in June of the following year, I borrowed my father's two-ton truck and showed up at Dundurn Castle in Hamilton at quarter to six each morning to pick up a motley crew of stout Ukrainian women ready to pick strawberries. I paid them five cents a quart. I was in business.

But first I had to find a place to sell my crop.

The biggest grocery store chain in Hamilton then was Loblaws, which is still Canada's biggest supermarket chain and food distributor. I went to the back entrance of the biggest Loblaws store in town, and asked to talk to the produce manager. I told him I had seven-and-a-half acres of fresh strawberries to sell.

"How much?" he asked. We struck a deal on the spot for twenty-five cents a quart. From that day on I was the main strawberry supplier for Loblaws, and provided strawberries for about half the one hundred ninety-five thousand people who lived in Hamilton.

By the second week of July, it was time to figure out if I had made a profit on my strawberry venture. After all the expenses and the loans to my father were paid, there was fourteen hundred dollars left on the table to split with my partners. I had earned seven hundred dollars for two summers' work, equivalent to about seven thousand in today's dollars. This was not a fortune, but at the time, it seemed a lot to me.

Is this a Horatio Alger story? Was it the first step in establishing a prosperous strawberry empire? Was I destined to become the straw-berry king of Ontario and live happily ever after? I'm afraid not. After all, I was only sixteen, and I began to be more interested in girls, ball-room dancing, and playing third base on the Millgrove softball team. So I took the money and ran.

But now, fifty-seven years later, I realize that my two years in the strawberry business gave me a deep appreciation of what it takes to run a small farm and make money doing it. This is at the very heart of my quest to find practical solutions to rural poverty over the past twenty-five years. The challenges, opportunities, and hard work I experienced in the strawberry business mirror the challenges one-acre farmers face every day as they try to make a living from their scattered quarter-acre plots.

And, of course, I realize now that I was practicing organic farming before it had a name.

I did just about all the work myself on those seven-and-a-half acres of strawberries, but I had access to horse-drawn plows, cultivators, and manure spreaders—a big advantage over most of the poor small-plot farmers in Africa now who, with no access to animal power, must plow, cultivate, and hoe by hand. Most of the world's poor small-acreage farmers remain far behind the animal-drawn level of mechanization I used on a small farm in Canada almost sixty years ago.

I learned a few other important things.

Although it was pretty hard for me to admit then, I learned that I couldn't go far in life without asking for help and getting it.

I learned that you can make a lot of money from a very small farm if you learn how to grow valuable crops, if you can find a market where you can sell them at a profit, if you have a good source for affordable plants and fertilizer, and if your crops don't get wiped out by diseases and pests.

I learned that learning new things every day brought me more pleasure and happiness than anything else I could do with my life.

I learned that the sun, wind, rain, and black root rot were pretty much beyond my control. I began to learn that giving up illusions of control might allow me to make a difference in the world far greater than that of which any King of Strawberries can dream.

It took thirty years for me to get involved in farming again. In the meantime I went to medical school, got married, became a psychiatrist, and ran businesses in real estate and in oil and gas. It was in 1981 that I became intrigued again with farming. This time, however, it was radically miniaturized hand-tool versions of farming, compared with the seven-acre strawberry farm I had reigned over. Now I began to learn everything I could about the one-acre farms where 800 million very poor people in the world had learned to survive on less than a dollar a day. That was the start of my quest to find ways they could earn much more from their tiny farms.

Many people ask me to explain why I stopped being a psychiatrist and changed over to working on poverty. But I don't really see it as a change. Because poverty plays such a critical role in the incidence and prevalence of all forms of illness, I have always believed that learning about poverty and what can be done to end it should be a basic science in every medical school and psychiatric-training curriculum. Thirty years ago, I became convinced that the most significant positive impact I could have on world health was to work on finding ways to end poverty.

I wish I could say that my work on poverty over the past twenty-five years has followed a carefully thought-out plan, but it was much more a process of jumping on opportunities that appeared unexpectedly and then learning from each experience. Of course, people make their own opportunities, and there was a strong element of that too. In my work as a psychiatrist, I discovered early on that I could learn more about the seriously mentally ill patients I was trying to help if I talked to them in their homes or their places of work, and if I listened to what they had to say.

One of the people I learned most from was Joe, who was both mentally ill and poor. When I became intrigued with the problem of homelessness, Maryanne Gleason, a friend who ran the Stout Street Clinic, which provided medical treatment for homeless people in Denver, introduced me to Joe, who had lived on the street for more than ten years, and he and I spent a day together. By the end of the day, I was stunned by how much I had learned. But it wouldn't have happened except that I approached learning about homelessness through three contrarian steps.

First, instead of interviewing Joe in my office, I talked to him in the three-foot-high space where he lived under a loading dock by the railroad tracks.

Second, I focused on learning about homelessness through Joe's eyes, instead of assuming I knew a lot about the subject already because I was a psychiatrist.

Third, I asked Joe to take me to the places where he lived his life, and I asked him every detail I could think of about each of them. We went together to the liquor store where he bought his beer and rotgut brandy, the railroad station where he stored his stuff in a locker, the outdoor roof under which he and his friends cooked their meals in a discarded charcoal grill, and to his home under a loading dock where he read books while tucked into his donated forty-below-zero sleeping bag before he turned off his lantern and went to sleep.

Maryanne set me up to meet Joe at a soup kitchen, where I was surprised to learn that he was one of their most reliable volunteers. I was dressed in ski clothes because it was a snowy day in December, and as soon as he saw me, Joe piled a white bread baloney sandwich and a bowl of soup on a depressing, industrial brown plastic tray and handed it to me. I was embarrassed. I said I had already had lunch, explained who I was, and asked if I could spend the afternoon with him.

"Sure, doc," he said, "if you don't mind waiting till I'm done with my shift."

So I read a book for half an hour till he was ready to go.

"I see you got a video camera, doc," he said. "Feel free to use it."

Our first stop was the railroad station.

"The first thing you need when you're homeless is a safe place to store your stuff," said Joe. "The train station lockers cost 75 cents for twenty-four hours, and that's a hell of a lot better than the bus station rip-off. There, they say it costs 75 cents; but if you come back an hour later, the meter says $2.50, and you can argue till you're blue in the face, and you still have to pay $2.50 to get your stuff back."

He dropped three quarters in the slot and pulled a bedroll and three bulging supermarket plastic bags out of his locker. I shot some footage of him pulling a can of pipe tobacco, spare socks, clean underwear, and a pint bottle of peppermint schnapps from one of his bags to show me. His bedroll was a heavy wool blanket tightly cinched with two leather belts around a good-quality, forty-below-zero sleeping bag.

It was snowing slightly as we trudged along the railroad tracks north of Union Station. Joe walked a little hunched over, with his feet slapping down into the snow one after the other. At the age of forty-five, with a full, trimmed black beard framed by a tightly fitting blue wool cap and wearing a padded red ski jacket drooping over a pair of clean but faded blue jeans tucked into leather hiking boots, he looked more like a rugged urban pioneer than a street bum. The third plastic shopping bag he was carrying contained a thermos of hot soup for his friend Chris, who had frostbitten toes and lived in a loading dock a quarter mile from Joe's. So we delivered Chris's soup and then we were off to Joe's home.

The entry to Joe's home under the loading dock was completely sealed off by three sheets of heavy black plastic, weighted down at the top by two big blocks of wood and at the bottom by three heavy rocks. Joe lived in an eight-by-ten-foot space a little over three feet high—I found that inside I could move like a crab if I stayed on my feet. But it was much easier moving around on my hands and knees. The floor was covered by a discarded carpet given to Joe by his rail yard worker friends, and a robust battery-powered lantern was suspended from a steel screw in the red brick wall at the back of the loading dock. Joe said he hung around with his friends in the afternoons, and after supper he climbed into his sleeping bag and read a book until he felt like going to sleep.

We went to the White Spot Café to talk. We drank a couple of cups of coffee while I ran the video camera. Joe left home when he was fourteen and started living on the streets. He joined the marines when he was seventeen, but went off the deep end and did the rounds of psych wards in VA hospitals for seven months, received a medical discharge, and hit the streets again. Five years ago he had ridden the rails to Denver, and that's where he had lived till now. From time to time, he became depressed, and when that happened, he went on medication provided by Stout Street Clinic.

"I don't like homeless shelters," he told me. "I've been to Jesus-Saves only three times in the last five years, and that was during my first month in Denver. It's not right. You have to listen to two hours of ear-banging by a preacher just to get one lousy free meal. I'd rather sleep out."

Joe lived on an income of about five hundred dollars a month. Sometimes he collected aluminum beer cans that he cashed in at the recycling center. He and a lot of his friends sold plasma at the blood bank. You were only supposed to do it once a month, but Joe often did it two or three times a week. He collected an occasional VA disability check, but more often than not, he didn't get it because he didn't have a legitimate address where it could be sent.

He could get a room in a fleabag hotel for two hundred dollars a month, but preferred to have some money for drinks and fun and sleep out. In his shoes, I think I would have done the same.

By the time Joe and I parted company, my head was spinning with ideas. Three thousand homeless people in Denver each spending $500 a month represented buying power of $1.5 million a month, a perfect opportunity to start grassroots businesses to serve the needs of the homeless. For example, why wouldn't homeless people be enthusiastic customers for a secure storage-locker enterprise owned and managed by other homeless people? Since many of the homeless smoked, why couldn't one or two of them get some tobacco, cigarette papers, and a cigarette-rolling machine, and start selling cigarettes? If so many of the homeless got medications paid for by the state at Stout Street Clinic, why wouldn't it be possible to set up a patient-owned pharmacy? (Dick Warner and I organized one in Boulder a year later, and it's now making a profit of $100,000 a year.)

What my afternoon with Joe confirmed for me is that coming up with practical solutions for homelessness requires going to the places where homeless people live, learning from them what their lives are like, why they do what they do, and what opportunities they take advantage of now and hope to take advantage of in the future. I was able to put what I had learned from my day with Joe to good use in learning about poverty by interviewing people all over the world who survive on less than a dollar a day, by walking with them through their one-acre farms and enjoying a cup of tea with their families, sitting on a stool in front of their thatched-roof mud-and-wattle homes.

These people told me they were poor because they couldn't earn enough from their one-acre farms. They said they needed access to affordable irrigation before they could grow the high-value crops that would increase their income, and sometimes they needed help to get these crops to markets where they could sell them at a profit. So in 1981 I started an organization called International Development Enterprises (IDE) that helped them meet these needs. We designed a range of affordable irrigation tools such as treadle pumps, and mass-marketed them to small-acreage farmers through the local private sector. We helped farmers pick four or five high-value fruits and vegetables they could grow well in their area, set up private-sector supply chains that sold them the seeds and fertilizer they needed to grow these crops, and helped them sell what they grew at a profit in the marketplace. This effectively ended the poverty of 17 million dollar-a-day rural people.

It has taken me twenty-five years to come to these ridiculously simple and obvious conclusions.

I've finally come to realize that seeing and doing the obvious is probably one of the most difficult things to do. I think that one of the influences that helped me to see and do the obvious—even if it took me twenty-five years to do it—is that my father was a survivor and one thing it takes to be a survivor is the capacity to see the world around you with open eyes.

By the time Neville Chamberlain gave the Sudetenland to Hitler as a gift, my father's plans to escape to Canada were almost complete. He told me later that the need to leave everything behind and escape was obvious. He said that since refugees, many with broken heads, had been streaming across the border with Germany for years, the disaster about to fall on us was predictable. He pleaded with his friends and relatives to escape before it was too late.

"But what would we do with the furniture?" they replied.

Most of them stayed in Czechoslovakia and died.

All too many times in my life I have encountered people who make disastrous mistakes because they keep their eyes closed to what is happening around them. Each time, I remember what my father's friends and relatives said when he pleaded with them to escape.

"But what would we do with the furniture?"

I think the furniture of our professional training—of the middle-class contexts in which most people from Europe, North America, and prosperous Asia are raised—contributes to our inability to see and do the obvious about poverty.

It may seem ridiculous to you for me to repeat each of the key things that I learned from talking to poor rural people—each of these points is so simple and obvious. But they're important enough that I'm going to do it anyway.

1. The biggest reason most poor people are poor is because they don't have enough money.

2. Most of the extremely poor people in the world earn their living now from one-acre farms.

3. They can earn much more money by finding ways to grow and sell high-value labor-intensive crops such as off-season fruits and vegetables.

4. To do that, they need access to very cheap small-farm irrigation, good seeds and fertilizer, and markets where they can sell their crops at a profit.

Any one of you can learn all of the above by spending one day in a poor village in any developing country and asking ten or twenty farmers why they are poor and what they can do about it. The remarkable thing is that poverty eradication programs continue to spend billions of dollars in poor countries, without much to show for it and without taking most of these points into account.

This book will describe in detail each of the steps needed to address these points, as well as the revolution in thinking and practice that is needed to end poverty, by telling the stories of the poor people I have met over the past twenty-five years.

Small-acreage farmers with their crop in Zambia

CHAPTER ONE

Twelve Steps to Practical Problem Solving

ONE OF THE THINGS THAT ALWAYS PIQUED MY CURIOSITY ABOUT poverty is that most people see it as more permanent than the Rock of Gibraltar. But I know that people are capable of moving out of poverty in a few months, because there are simple and obvious solutions to it. The central theme of this book is that you can come up with obvious practical solutions to just about any complicated social problem by following a few simple basic steps. Here are the twelve steps I used to arrive at the solutions to extreme poverty I describe in this book. Although each of them is simple and obvious, many people find them difficult to apply. For example, most poverty experts spend little or no time talking with and listening to extremely poor people in the places where they live and work, although that is exactly where I have been guided to most of the practical solutions to poverty that I describe in this book.

1. Go to where the action is.

2. Talk to the people who have the problem and listen to what they say.

3. Learn everything you can about the problem's specific context.

4. Think big and act big.

5. Think like a child.

6. See and do the obvious.

7. If somebody has already invented it, you don't need to do so again.

8. Make sure your approach has positive measurable impacts that can be brought to scale. Make sure it can reach at least a million people and make their lives measurably better.

9. Design to specific cost and price targets.

10. Follow practical three-year plans.

11. Continue to learn from your customers.

12. Stay positive: don't be distracted by what other people think.

1. GO TO WHERE THE ACTION IS

You can't sit in your office at the World Bank or in your research lab at Stanford and figure out what to do about poverty in Myanmar.

Hurricane Katrina struck New Orleans at 6:10 a.m. on August 29, 2005. Here's what Michael Brown, director of the Federal Emergency Management Agency (FEMA) said when Paula Zahn, a CNN interviewer, asked him four days later about the desperate conditions where crowds of people had sought refuge at the Ernest N. Morial Convention Center.

Michael Brown: "We just learned about that today."

Paula Zahn: "Sir, you're not telling me… that you just learned that the folks at the convention center didn't have food and water until today, are you?"

Brown: "Paula, the federal government did not even know about the convention center people until today."[1]

What kept Michael Brown from going to the convention center to see for himself? The practical solutions for the rapidly deteriorating conditions experienced by so many Katrina survivors who had taken shelter there would have been immediately obvious.

Michael Brown resigned under pressure a few weeks later.

In 1981, when I was working on a project to build and sell five hundred donkey carts to refugees in Somalia, I met a pleasant middle-aged man who managed five health clinics in refugee camps for a major international relief organization.

"How often do you get out to the refugee camps to visit your clinics?" I asked.

"I haven't been there yet and I don't plan to go soon," he said with considerable pride. "If you go to the field, it's mass confusion. Managers have to be able to think clearly, without distractions, to make good decisions, and you simply can't do it in the middle of the noise and chaos of field conditions."

I was so astonished that for once in my life I was speechless.

Two months ago, I had lunch with a man who managed a large US-based demonstration farm for an organization that makes livestock available to poor rural families in developing countries. He was responsible for public education and fund-raising with the thousands of people who visited the farm each year. During the seven years he had managed this important demonstration farm, he had never visited any of his organization's programs in developing countries.

I simply can't imagine how anybody can make realistic plans to eradicate poverty or to address any important problem without visiting the places where the problem is occurring and talking with the people who have the problem.

2. TALK TO THE PEOPLE WHO HAVE THE PROBLEM, AND LISTEN TO WHAT THEY HAVE TO SAY

In the 1990s, agriculture experts in Bangladesh were dismayed that small-acreage farmers were applying only a tiny fraction of the fertilizer that their monsoon-season rice crops needed, even though they could triple their investment in fertilizer from the increased rice yields the recommended amount would stimulate. The experts complained about the irrational and superstitious behavior of small-acreage farmers, and set up extension programs and farmer-training programs, but nothing worked. The farmers continued to apply a tiny fraction of the fertilizer that their rice needed to thrive. Finally, somebody asked some farmers why they were using so little fertilizer.

"Oh, that's easy," they said. "Every ten years or so around here, there is a major flood during the monsoon season that carries away all the fertilizer we apply. So we only apply the amount of fertilizer we can afford to lose in a ten-year flood."

Suddenly it became clear that the farmers were excellent, rational decision makers and that it was the agriculture experts who had a lot to learn. In order to survive, subsistence farmers have to be at the cutting edge of avoiding risk. With very good reason, they care much more about avoiding losing their farm than they do about tripling their income. When they have the opportunity (and the money) to invest in fertilizer during the dry season when the risk of floods is close to zero, they are glad to do so.

There is another problem with this action step. Far too many people can talk to the people who have the problem and not learn anything, because those who would help don't always know how to listen. As a young psychiatrist in 1962, I got interested in finding out if the patients admitted to the psychiatric wards of Colorado Mental Health Institute at Fort Logan and the psychiatrists, social workers, and nurses treating them were working on the same treatment goals. To my amazement, the mental health professionals not only had different treatment goals from their patients, but they also were unable to predict which goals the patients saw as most important. When I asked more questions, I learned that mental health professionals were trained to define the problem bringing a patient to a psychiatric hospital as a mental illness inside the head of the patient, while patients saw the problem as residing in the group of people with whom they lived and worked outside the hospital. Often the patient's symptoms of mental illness would get better when he or she was given medication and removed from the upheavals going on in his or her real-life setting, only to be readmitted to hospital after being released again into the unchanged social setting that had precipitated the symptoms in the first place. When mental health professionals learned to listen for and intervene in the problems in the real-life setting at the same time they diagnosed the symptoms of mental illness, treatment outcome improved dramatically. The same kind of thing happens with people trying to address the problems of poverty. If these professionals are trained to assume that modern farming depends on Western mechanization, in the end they are likely to leave behind rusting hulks of big tractors and harvesters as monuments to the inability to listen and learn.

3. LEARN EVERYTHING YOU CAN ABOUT THE PROBLEM'S SPECIFIC CONTEXT

We achieved a great deal of success with treadle pumps in Bangladesh. Now I quickly run out of fingers and toes when I try to count how many people have asked me if they could use treadle pumps to help farmers in villages in other countries.

"How deep is the water table in your village?" I ask, because a treadle pump is a suction pump that simply won't lift water more than about twenty-seven feet.

"I don't know" is the most common answer.

"Tie a rock on the end of a piece of string, go to the nearest well, and measure how deep the water table is," I say. "Or go to the government ministry of water resources—they likely have maps with that kind of information."

"OK, we'll do it the next time we visit," they say.

The fact is, you can't make practical plans unless you gather a lot of details about each specific village context. What kind of high-value crops you can grow in each depends on the type of soil and the climate. The price of fruits and vegetables is usually highest at the time of year when it's most difficult to grow them, so it's important to know why these crops are difficult to grow at that time of year and what can be done to overcome the difficulty. If there is a factory nearby with jobs that pay well, the labor required for intensive horticulture may be hard to come by.

Everything I have to say in this book depends almost totally on having interviewed three thousand poor farm families, listened carefully to what they had to say, and learned everything I could about the specific context in which they lived and worked.

4. THINK BIG AND ACT BIG

If you learn about a problem in its real-life context from the people who have the problem, ask basic questions, and open your eyes to see the obvious, you are likely to come up with big ideas with world-changing potential. This is not only exhilarating, it can be frightening —and some people react to this excitement by making puny action plans. Other people fail to think and act big because they have never done so and aren't used to it, or because they don't want to be seen as arrogant, or because they are afraid of failing if they think too big. I have learned to look at the total global market potential of any idea from the beginning, even if doing so makes me uncomfortable. I've gotten used to the grandiosity labels that come with thinking big.

In the chapter on creating new markets, I will consider the fact that there are a billion people in the world who need eyeglasses but don't have them, and I will discuss the potential solution of providing access to display stands from which people could pick two-dollar spectacles that correct their vision problems. When most people think of implementing a solution like this, they think small. There are several organizations that have started to provide affordable reading glasses to poor people, but all of them together have delivered less than a half million eyeglasses, which serves less than one-tenth of 1 percent of the customers who need them. I start by thinking about how to reach half of the total potential market of 1 billion or so within fifteen years. A business plan to accomplish this would probably need to reach global sales of 50 million a year within five years, purchasing fifty-cent eyeglasses from mainland China a million or more at a time and selling them at a retail price of about two dollars. I would spend most of my time designing an effective global marketing-and-distribution plan for both rural and urban areas, and wrap it up with a clear statement of the start-up capital required to implement a three-year plan, how it would be spent, and what it would accomplish. This kind of planning is routine for large businesses or for any entrepreneur seeking start-up venture capital, but it is rare for development organizations.

Thinking big in this way always carries the risk that you will fail in a big way. But if you can't stand to take the risk of failing and looking bad while doing so, you probably should be in a different line of work.

If you want to make the world a better place, coming up with a breakthrough concept or technology is just the first step. The most challenging problem is coming up with a practical way that you can put the innovation into the hands of the hundreds of millions of people in the world who need it.

5. THINK LIKE A CHILD

Coming from a refugee family who barely escaped being murdered by Hitler in Czechoslovakia in 1939 when I was five-and-a-half, I don't want to romanticize childhood. But there is a simple and direct curiosity in childhood and a love of play that we tend to miss badly in our approach to problem-solving as adults. If you think like a child, you can quickly strip a problem down to its basic elements.

In 1996 I was in Cachoeira, the Amazon rain forest home village of Chico Mendes, who founded the rubber tappers' union and was martyred by the cattle interests. I was trying to figure out how rubber tappers could shell and dry Brazil nuts at the village gathering point so they could increase their income. We had to design a village drier to replace the large industrial driers of big-city plants. When we walked through rain forest villages, I saw that every second house had a *forno de farinha,* a two-foot-high baked-clay furnace with an eight-by-ten-foot stove top used to dry manioc flour. When I saw all these ovens used to dry manioc, I realized that each of them could also become a Brazil nut drier. If you think about how to dry something as if you're a child instead of an engineer, you think about how you can warm it and blow air over it, like when you hang a wet towel on a clothesline in the breeze and the sunlight.

So we built a removable wooden house with a chimney that sat on top of the manioc-drying oven, and used the heat coming from the stove top to draw air over the surface of Brazil nuts that were drying on wire-mesh drawers inside the wooden house. We built the first one from scratch in two hours.

6. SEE AND DO THE OBVIOUS

If we can't see our blind spots, how can we begin to see and do the obvious?

Here is an obvious fact that hasn't been incorporated into the plans of most poverty alleviation experts. It took me several years and several hundred interviews with poor families to begin to see it. Three-quarters of the dollar-a-day poverty in the world has its roots in tiny farms. Ninety-eight percent of all the farms in China, 96 percent of the farms in Bangladesh, 87 percent of the farms in Ethiopia, and 80 percent of the farms in India are smaller than five acres. Eight hundred million of the people who earn less than a dollar a day scratch most of what they earn out of one-acre farms that are divided into four or five scattered quarter-acre plots. International Development Enterprises (IDE), the small organization I started, has been able to help 17 million people out of poverty because we realized that creating new wealth on one-acre farms depends on opening access to new forms of irrigation, agriculture, markets, and design.

7. IF SOMEBODY HAS ALREADY INVENTED IT, YOU DON'T NEED TO DO SO AGAIN

People are often hesitant to use ideas from elsewhere. I have run into countless instances of the not-invented-here syndrome. Doing a quick world search to see if somebody has already come up with a solution to the problem you're working on is always faster and easier than coming up with something new.

Perhaps the most embarrassing example of learning that it had already been invented came when I was convinced that I had found a new way of delivering water cheaply, drop by drop, to plants by punching holes in plastic pipes and letting water slowly dribble out. Dan Spare, the first engineer I talked to about this great of idea of mine, politely informed me that the Israelis had invented it thirty-five years earlier and that it was called "drip irrigation." I had never heard of it.

So I scanned the world literature on drip irrigation and learned that while the method had spread rapidly, it represented only 1 percent of irrigated acreage, because the setup was too big and too expensive for the majority of the world's farmers. So we went to work to design drip-irrigation systems that cut existing costs by four-fifths, reducing their size to fit small plots.

8. MAKE SURE YOUR APPROACH HAS POSITIVE MEASURABLE IMPACTS THAT CAN BE BROUGHT TO SCALE

While we were working on the donkey cart project in Somalia, we ran across a team from International Labor Organization (ILO) that had organized a project to help refugee women make and sell soap. But when we asked how much it would cost to buy some of this soap, it was hard to get a clear answer. We eventually learned that ILO could have bought the finest, most perfumed soaps available in Paris, air-freighted them to Somalia, and sold them at a cheaper price than what it cost to produce the crude soap the refugees were making with ILO's help. When I asked how she could justify this, the program's manager hinted that I had no understanding of the tremendous importance of the self-esteem these women gained from the positive group interaction during the process of making the soap.

On the contrary, I believed that the only real self-esteem raised by this project was that of the ladies in the project team that designed and implemented it. If they were really interested in improving the self-esteem of the refugee women with whom they worked, they would help these women produce something they could continue selling at a profit long after ILO left Somalia. Producing soap at a cost greater than the existing market price for the finest soaps also meant that the project would be unlikely ever to be taken up by other groups of women, so it could never be expanded beyond its original scope.

How many people can benefit from a development project if it proves to be successful? This is one of the first questions to be asked about any idea for a practical solution, since it takes a lot of time and money to implement a project. But often this question is never asked. For example, a few refugees in Somalia who lived in camps beside rivers and caught catfish to sell could broaden their markets by preserving the fish through salting and smoking, since refrigeration was unavailable. But all refugees needed affordable transport services, so picking between fish smokers and donkey carts was a no-brainer.

The only projects worth doing have measurable costs, impacts that are an improvement over their antecedents, and the potential to be brought to scale.

9. DESIGN TO SPECIFIC COST AND PRICE TARGETS

The key issue that prevented the ILO staff from implementing a cost-effective project is that they had little interest in figuring out the cost and price targets refugee women had to reach to be competitive in the local marketplace. Like so many other development organizations, they scorned materialistic measurements such as costs and profits, and had no measurements of impact other than their own belief that the group activity was good for refugee morale.

10. FOLLOW PRACTICAL THREE-YEAR PLANS

You may have a world-changing plan with a stunning vision for the future, but if you can't come up with a specific plan for the next three-year period, you'll never get anywhere. If your three-year targets are too ambitious, you will likely fail long before you have any chance of reaching your long-range vision. If your three-year targets are too puny, you won't lay a solid base for scaling up. As in "Goldilocks and the Three Bears," your three-year objectives have to be not too big, not too small, but just right.

When I wrote a three-page concept note for the Bill and Melinda Gates Foundation, I said that my long-term vision was to increase the net yearly income of 30 million families by five hundred dollars a year, and the foundation was satisfied. But when we started negotiating a specific initiative they could support, they said "Forget the 30 million —we want to see clear evidence over the next four years that you can reach 100,000. Prove to us that you can achieve the specific impacts that you say you can, and then we can consider going on to phase two and maybe even phase three."

11. CONTINUE TO LEARN FROM YOUR CUSTOMERS

About ten years ago, the low-cost drip-irrigation technology we designed and field-tested in Nepal was ready for marketing. By this time we had a good sales force, and several hundred hill farmers within thirty kilometers of Pokhara purchased low-cost drip systems. But sales didn't go up at all in the second year. In fact, our field staff were dismayed to learn that many farmers who bought low-cost drip systems used only a quarter of the system they purchased. When they interviewed the farmers who had bought drip systems, our field staff learned these were maize and millet farmers who had no experience with the intensive horticulture required to grow off-season vegetables. In fact, there was a widely held belief that it was impossible to grow vegetables in winter in the Pokhara region, which became a self-fulfilling prophecy.

Our Pokhara field staff convinced the Kathmandu office staff, who convinced me, that we would never be able to sell low-cost drip systems until we trained farmers how to use these systems to grow off-season vegetables. We introduced field-based training programs in intensive horticulture, and sales took off quickly. It never would have happened if our field staff hadn't kept talking to our customers.

Each of the last twenty-five years, I have interviewed at least a hundred of IDE's small-acreage customers. All my ideas for projects that worked, and even some that didn't work, came from what I learned from these small-acreage farmers, and now all the people who work for IDE talk to and learn from these farmers every day.

12. STAY POSITIVE: DON'T BE DISTRACTED BY WHAT OTHER PEOPLE THINK

Twelve years ago I was championing two affordable irrigation technologies. The first was an animal-powered treadle pump, which produced as much water as a small diesel pump. A lot of people told me that if an animal-driven treadle pump putting out five liters of water a second were needed, it would have been developed long ago. I ignored them. A five-horsepower diesel pump cost $500 then, and I knew we could produce a bullock pump for $125, a pump that "burned" fodder instead of diesel. So I kept pressing till we had a marketable reliable bullock pump ready to go.

At the same time, I was convinced that a small-plot drip-irrigation system that could be bought at about a fifth of the price of conventional drip would command huge global demand. People told me if there really were a need for such a system, the market would have introduced it long ago. But I was convinced that millions of small-acreage farmers could earn big money from drip-irrigated vegetables. It took seven years to bring the first low-cost drip systems to market.

By the time the bullock pump was ready to sell, Chinese diesel pumps were available for one hundred fifty dollars instead of the five-hundred-dollar price farmers paid two years earlier, and the bullock pump was no longer cost-competitive. I had no regrets. We had good reasons to develop the bullock pump, and we had good reasons at that point to put the product on a back burner. The global market for low-cost drip irrigation, however, looks to be huge. I think at least 10 million poor families will buy a system.

Most breakthrough solutions to important problems, such as Henry Ford's five-hundred-dollar automobile and Jobs and Wozniak's two-thousand-dollar computer, came about because one or two stubborn entrepreneurs saw new solutions to old problems and persisted until their dream became a reality. Why should solving the problem of poverty be any different?

I have set a target for IDE of ending the poverty of 30 million dollar-a-day families by the year 2020 by using these twelve principles, and I'm sure we'll make it.

Unclogging a plugged emitter in a low-cost drip irrigation system in Nepal

Low-cost drip irrigation in Zimbabwe

CHAPTER TWO

The Three
Great Poverty
Eradication Myths

I LEARNED QUICKLY THAT THE BEST WAY TO SATISFY MY CURIOS-
ity about poverty is to have long conversations with poor people in the
places where they live and work and dream, and to listen to what they
have to say. This means talking to one-acre farmers who live on less
than a dollar a day, and walking with them through their fields. I left
Kathmandu in fall of 2001 on a jeep trip that led to my first meeting
with Krishna Bahadur Thapa, his two wives, and their three children
in the tiny hill village of Ekle Phant in Nepal.

While two fuzzy-cheeked youths in drab green army uniforms,
Kalashnikovs slung over their shoulders, riffled through our driver's
documents, Bob Nanes, Deepak Adhikari, and I continued to argue
about something so trivial that we forgot what it was before the argu-
ment ended. We had been stopped just outside Kathmandu at one of
the numerous army checkpoints that had sprung up in response to
Maoist rebel activities.

Bob Nanes is a classic contrarian: if you say "black," he says "white."
No surprise that we were arguing about nothing. In any case, his

contrary nature was one of the things that led me to appoint him as
the director of International Development Enterprises' programs in
Nepal. I started IDE to help poor people increase their income. That
has been its goal throughout its existence.

Deepak Adhikari speaks Russian fluently because he spent five
years in Moscow on a scholarship getting his engineering degree.
Deepak will give you a one-hour creative lecture on horseflies or anything else you care to mention, if you don't stop him. He is in charge
of coming up with breakthrough affordable irrigation tools, a hot topic
for most Nepali farmers.

We were on our way to talk to thirty or forty one-acre-farm families in the hills of Nepal who bought and installed IDE low-cost drip
systems eighteen months earlier to irrigate off-season cauliflower and
cucumbers. I was eager to learn how much money they had made and
what problems they had encountered.

After two-and-a-half bone-jarring hours dodging potholes big
enough to sink our jeep, we turned west at Mugling and crossed the
bridge over the boiling Trisuli River. A few minutes later we stopped
in a small clearing in the village of Ekle Phant, where eight or nine
farm families stood shyly in the shade of a tree, waiting to greet us.
They had been forewarned and knew that I was likely to ask a lot of
impertinent questions, so they offered up Krishna Bahadur Thapa as a
sacrificial lamb to my curiosity. He was a sturdy fifty-six-year-old man
with a weather-beaten bronzed face who looked as if he could take on
the whole Nepali army with one hand tied behind his back, and do it
with a smile.

Bahadur and two of his neighbors took us on a leisurely stroll over
rolling fields to his home, a pleasant three-room typical stone-and-
plaster hill cottage. There, his oldest wife, Padam Maya Magar, forty-
six, greeted us with a steaming copper pot of tea. What I didn't learn
till later is that Bahadur had a second wife, Devi Maya Magar, his first
wife's sister. (It is acceptable in some Nepal hill village cultures for a
man to take a second wife if he has no children with the first.) Bahadur and his second wife had two sons, Deu, twenty-five, and Puspa,
twenty-one.

I blew on my tea and sipped it. Many visitors to rural villages refuse
to eat anything because they don't want to get sick, but I learned early

on that anything steaming is likely to be safe to consume. A more practical question is how to get rid of five or ten cups of tea. It is perfectly acceptable there for a man to step aside and relieve himself by a cornfield while the group keeps talking, but women are expected to be private, so most experienced female visitors simply keep a firm limit on the amount of tea they drink during these visits.

Bahadur had inherited two acres of scattered fields. He had one acre of rain-fed monsoon rice, by the river half a mile from his house, which was producing twelve hundred fifty kilos of traditional rice, enough to feed his family most years and make fifty to a hundred dollars from selling their surplus. On the acre of scattered upland plots close to their house, they rotated black gram, a low-value beanlike pulse, maize, and some monsoon vegetables for the table. In years when the rice crop wasn't good, Bahadur's family ran out of food for a few months before the monsoon harvest came in. To make ends meet, he and his two sons looked for seasonal work in Mugling, and sometimes in Kathmandu, which could earn another one hundred dollars, enough to buy the food they needed.

For me, the best part of talking with small-farm families comes when they get comfortable enough to speak about their dreams. Bahadur and his family's fondest dream was to find some way they could earn much more income from their small farm. With more income, they could buy the food they needed. They could give their children a better education. They could buy medicines, buy more land, and perhaps invest in a cow and a buffalo and start selling milk.

The catch was, they had no idea how they could squeeze more income out of their farm. They didn't know how they could produce more rice or black gram to sell, and even if they were to double their production, they couldn't see a way to earn more than two hundred dollars a year from selling surplus rice, corn, or beans, and that would still leave them on the edge of survival.

The main question Bahadur asked us was left unanswered, and it's the same question that had haunted me for years. What could Bahadur and his family do to move out of poverty? They had two acres—more than many of the families of Ekle Phant—they were hard workers, and they were willing to do just about anything.

Was there anything we could do to help them?

This is the central question of this book.

There are some 800 million people in the world who, like Bahadur and his family, live in rural areas in developing countries and make their living from small farms. The scattered quarter-acre plots where they scratch out a living usually have poor soil and no access to irrigation. Their main crops are rice, wheat, and corn, but they usually can't produce enough to keep from going hungry. If they grow rice, wheat, or corn to sell in the market, the price is too low to clear more than two hundred dollars an acre, not nearly enough to move these families out of poverty.

There are some simple solutions to this problem. Sadly, the people in charge of the world's poverty programs rarely focus on simple solutions, and the monumental investments made in poverty eradication initiatives have at best produced meager results.

"We have invested a staggering $568 billion in development aid in Africa over the past forty-two years, and have very little to show for it," says William Easterly, formerly a senior economist at the World Bank. Over those same forty-two years, the per capita growth rate of the median African nation has stayed close to zero.[2, 3]

While not quite as bleak as in sub-Saharan Africa, the track record of aid to developing countries in other parts of the world has been far from stellar. Between 1950 and 1970, major investments in developing countries were in dams, schools, roads, and other infrastructure improvements. While this created some positive impacts on poverty, the number of gigantic projects with poor returns on investment led to the debt crises and loan forgiveness of the 1980s.[4] An ensuing round of development investment attempted to replicate the economic success of Korea and the East Asian tigers. But addressing price distortions, opening trade, and correcting budget deficits in structural adjustment loans created another load of debt that could not be repaid, ending in 100 percent cancellation of loans in the Multilateral Debt Relief Initiative in 2006.[5]

The current "answer to poverty" is the UN-sponsored Millennium Development Goals initiative, led by Jeffrey Sachs and backed by 189 governments. This highly publicized initiative plans to make dramatic improvements by the year 2015 in eradication of poverty and hunger; access to water and sanitation; decrease in child and maternal mortality;

gender equity; prevention of the spread of malaria, tuberculosis, and HIV/AIDS; cessation of environmental degradation; debt relief; access to information technology; and the status of landlocked and island states. All of this will be accomplished by doing much more of essentially the same things we have been doing until now.

In 2004, about the midpoint in the 1990–2015 time period for accomplishing all this, the World Economic Forum in Davos concluded that efforts toward achieving the UN's Millennium Development Goals were faltering badly.[6] After a year of study, the forum's Global Governance Initiative rated progress on each goal from one to ten. They gave progress on eradication of poverty a rating of four, attributed mainly to domestic policies and private efforts. They rated lessening of hunger at three, improvement of education at three, and improvements in environment at three, health at four, and human rights at three.

In light of the importance of the Millennium Development Goals to halve hunger and poverty, at the halfway point the progress on reaching these goals is even more discouraging. The 2006 report of this initiative[7] on progress in halving the percentage of people in sub-Saharan Africa who live on less than a dollar a day provides convincing evidence to support Easterly's contention that we have little to show for our massive investments in development aid in Africa.

From 1990 to 2002, the percentage of dollar-a-day people in sub-Saharan Africa, where most of the people in Africa live, stayed at around 44 percent (see Table 1), and the absolute number of very poor people increased by 140 million. In sub-Saharan Africa, we are moving backward in our attempts to eradicate poverty.

Things look a little better for dollar-a-day poverty in other developing countries. Between 1990 and 2002, the percentage of people in developing regions who survive on less than a dollar a day dropped from 27.9 percent to 19.4 percent.[10] A large proportion of this reported decrease came from China and its billion-plus population, where the percentage of dollar-a-day people dropped from 33 percent in 1990 to 17 percent in 2001,[11] halving the percentage of extremely poor people. But the drop in poverty in China did not come about because of give-away programs implemented by the Millennium Development initiative, but because the government of China reversed the disastrous agricultural policies implemented under Mao which caused the deaths of 40 million people by starvation. After such a disaster, just about any change will be better, but the decollectivization movement led by Deng Xiao Peng and many others allowed small-acreage farmers to start producing for the market, and this stimulated economic growth in rural areas where poor small-acreage farmers earned their livelihoods, bringing many people out of poverty. It also created the basis for the export-based coastal development zones that were largely responsible for China's continuing national economic growth. But this national economic growth centered in China is strikingly uneven geographically.

China is really at least two separate countries. The first country—centered in the coastal belt with nearly ideal climate, soil, water, and transport conditions—used a prosperous agricultural base to launch an export-oriented economic miracle taking advantage of low-cost labor.

The second country, centered in the remote Yellow River valley regions of northwest China, has optimal conditions for continuing poverty—overpopulation; poor soils; high erosion; low rainfall; poor transport, trade, and communications; and very low agricultural productivity. These areas are populated by millions and millions of families eking out a living on half an acre of land leased from the government.

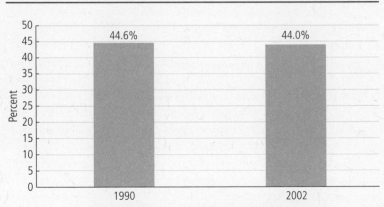

Percentage of people in sub-Saharan Africa living on $1 a day

Table 1: Impact of Development Aid in Sub-Saharan Africa[8, 9]

At the toughest times of the year, some of the families in remote parts of Gansu and Janxi provinces have to survive on food and water brought in at significant cost by the government. The prosperity of the first country has had very little impact on the poverty of the second.

Of course, China's economic miracle has had some positive impact on the poor in remote areas in China's northwest. I visited a prosperous vegetable-processing and -freezing plant two hours west of Shanghai. One thousand women from poor areas in northwest China were bused in every three months, housed on site, and paid to cut cauliflower and other vegetables into tiny pieces that were frozen and shipped to make pizza toppings in Japan and the United States. They earned forty dollars a month on top of their transport and per diem expenses, which proved useful to their families in poor villages in provinces like Gansu and Janxi. But this level of income contributed only a little to ending their poverty. Further poverty reduction in China will depend on creating economic growth in northwest China and its other remote, poor rural regions.

The increase in the percentage of poor people in sub-Saharan Africa over the next twelve years is likely to be equal to or greater than further reductions that are apt to occur in Eastern Asia and other developing regions. This makes it extremely unlikely that the goal of halving dollar-a-day poverty will be achieved.

It is even more unlikely that the related Millennium goal on hunger will be achieved. Between 1990 and 2002, the percentage of people who are always hungry decreased only from 20 percent to 17 percent, and the absolute number of hungry people increased by 4 million per year between 1995 and 2000,[12] reaching 824 million by 2002.[13] Since the root cause of hunger is poverty and one of the first things poor people do with new income is buy the food they need to end their hunger, how is it that hunger has remained essentially unchanged if there has been some drop in extreme poverty?

The 2006 progress report of the Millennium initiative concludes that the goal to double the percentage of people with access to sanitation likely will not be reached.[14]

I believe that with business as usual, we have little hope of achieving most of the Millennium Development Goals.

Perhaps our biggest problem is that our thinking about poverty and what can be done to end it is severely hobbled by three great poverty eradication myths.

The Three Great Poverty Eradication Myths

WE CAN DONATE PEOPLE OUT OF POVERTY

The most important poverty eradication myth is that we can donate people out of poverty. Incredibly, Jeff Sachs, the head of the UN Millennium Development Goals initiative, believes that people who live on a dollar a day are too poor to invest their own money to move out of poverty. So he and the development experts he leads are asking for $160 billion a year for ten years, primarily as gifts from rich countries to poor countries, to build the missing infrastructure that will allow economic growth to take off in poor rural areas, which in turn will end dollar-a-day poverty. This is simply another version of the massive investments in infrastructure made between 1950 and 1970 that required the loan forgiveness of the 1980s. Although the Millennium Development Goals are admirable and impressive, the strategies to achieve them are fatally flawed—big infrastructure investments, big agriculture projects, big irrigation, and big budgets controlled by the governments of developing countries—all efforts that bypass poor rural people eking out a living on one-acre farms. These are exactly the same things that have failed repeatedly in the past.

Here is what will really happen. Western "experts" with little or no exposure to the village will decide how to spend the money. As soon as word gets out that a multimillion-dollar giveaway is coming, developing-country politicians with Swiss bank accounts and get-rich-quick businessmen will gather like moths around a flame. They will participate in congratulatory ribbon-cutting ceremonies. For the first year or two, generously funded big projects will produce excellent results— exemplary yields of grain, for example, created by big investments in inputs and modern machinery supervised by well-paid Western consultants—and will receive dramatic media coverage. But when the project money runs out, yields will drop back to normal. Any positive impacts of investments at the village level will be outweighed by market distortions from project-induced corruption and subsidies, sabotaging the emergence of true markets. Poor people will appreciate having had a free ride for a time, knowing all along that it would never last. After the grand gifting period is over, media silence will descend on the village, and most poor villagers will be worse off than before. This failure will provide more ammunition for those who believe there is no practical solution to poverty. It will become harder to raise money for projects that actually work.

This is not a new scenario. It has been enacted thousands of times in poor villages, although not on quite as grand a scale as that recommended by Jeff Sachs and his colleagues. Many organizations have donated village hand pumps to provide clean drinking water to village families, only to return two years later to find that 80 percent of them were not working—because nobody had assumed ownership, so when the pumps broke, nobody fixed them.

In the 1970s, the World Bank invested some $35 million US in projects to install deep and shallow diesel-pump irrigation tube wells in Bangladesh. At that time, just after the war of independence, Bangladesh needed to increase national food production, which dictated a major increase in irrigated acreage. The Bank gave loans at such low rates of interest to the government of Bangladesh that they amounted to an 85 percent subsidy. The Bangladesh government in turn passed on this generosity to richer farmers who could afford to pay bribes.

The shallow tube wells funded by this project were capable of irrigating fifteen acres, and farmers were given loans to buy them from local banks. The farmers who got them paid bribes to the government officials responsible for distributing them. Then the farmers dutifully defaulted on the loans guaranteed by the government of Bangladesh, which, of course, never paid back the loans to the World Bank, and everyone involved knew that this would happen from the beginning.

The deep tube wells could irrigate one hundred acres, and were given to farmers at zero cost, which meant that they had to pay bigger bribes to get them. One of the problems that the World Bank and government experts never anticipated is that because farms in Bangladesh are so fragmented, there were fifty or more farmers in the twelve-to-fifteen-acre command area of a shallow tube well, and hundreds in the hundred-acre command area of the deep tube well. This significantly increased the complexity of water distribution.

Not surprisingly, a typical shallow tube well ended up irrigating four or five acres instead of its fifteen-acre capacity, and deep tube wells rarely irrigated forty acres of their one-hundred-acre capacity. A more sinister problem was that the richer farmers who could get mechanized pumps became water lords, sold water at exorbitant prices to poor farmers, foreclosed their loans, and seized their land. The rich got richer, and the poor got poorer. Because they weren't financially sustainable, most of the deep tube wells were abandoned when the subsidy ran out. Because they were smaller and cheaper, the shallow tube wells proved profitable from the beginning, and they continued making rich farmers richer. Of course, the goal of expanding national irrigated acreage was achieved—but much less acreage came under irrigation than the experts predicted.

At about the same time, poor farmers began buying much smaller and cheaper manually powered treadle pumps introduced by the Rangpur Dinajpur Rural Service (RDRS), a Lutheran-sponsored rural development organization, and mass-marketed by IDE. Most development and irrigation leaders in Bangladesh agreed that these small, low-cost pumps produced a much more positive impact on poverty alleviation and social justice, but because each one irrigated only half an acre, irrigation experts were convinced that only the bigger pumps could put enough land under irrigation to grow the rice the nation needed.

Twelve years later, 1.5 million poor farmers had purchased treadle pumps at an unsubsidized market price of $25 and placed seven hundred fifty thousand new acres under irrigation in Bangladesh at a fraction of the $35 million (US) public cost of the World Bank project that provided larger-acreage farmers with shallow and deep tube wells at no cost other than the bribes they had to pay to government officials to receive them.

In the late 1980s, when treadle pumps were becoming increasingly popular, Bangladesh's president, Hossain Mohammad Ershad, announced a few months before election time that he would donate twenty thousand of them to his home province. Farmers there immediately stopped buying and waited for free treadle pumps to appear. Many small-volume manufacturers, dealers, and well-drillers in the region went out of business. The government gave the treadle pump contract to a large-volume manufacturer with political connections who never had made treadle pumps, and he produced two thousand or so of very poor quality. The promised twenty thousand treadle pumps never came, and thousands of farmers who could have cleared one hundred dollars a year on an investment of twenty-five dollars to buy a treadle pump lost big.

But giveaways and subsidies are not limited to ambitious global poverty programs. They are often enthusiastically supported by large corporations.

A few years ago I spent a week in Israel trying to form a partnership with Netafim, the biggest drip-irrigation company in the world, with the hope that IDE and Netafim could collaborate to develop and mass-market a line of extremely affordable drip-irrigation equipment to tens of millions of small-acreage farmers.

No dice.

Netafim's directors believe they make the best drip-irrigation equipment in the world. They wanted to stay with higher-margin products even if a larger-volume market was available at a lower price. They were worried that they might ruin their reputation for excellence if they started making lower-cost equipment.

"Poor farmers deserve the best equipment," they said. "Let's form a partnership to win big World Bank contracts in Africa. The World Bank can easily subsidize the cost of our drip-irrigation equipment to a price poor farmers can afford. This will allow them to use the best drip equipment in the world, just like rich farmers. Netafim's sales will increase, and IDE will gain access to World Bank funding to expand its poverty alleviation initiatives."

Doesn't this sound attractive? Netafim gets a nice bump in sales. IDE gets access to World Bank funding. Farmers with connections get access to high-quality drip irrigation at a bargain price. The only problem is that it's a lousy deal for poor small-acreage farmers. The global demand for low-cost drip irrigation is far too big to provide these nice subsidies for everybody, so the people who get them are the ones with connections and bribes for government officials. In the meantime, the people who get cut out of this comfortable game are the small-acreage farmers who earn less than a dollar a day. What's more, subsidies on price pull the rug out from under small-scale entrepreneurs trying to make a living fabricating and selling affordable irrigation to farmers. But in the end, it all gets sold to the public as another successful poverty program.

As you can probably guess, I left Israel without making a deal with Netafim.

But this type of subsidy solution is endemic in the development world. It's used by governments, the World Bank, UNICEF, the United Nations, politicians, and many development leaders who look for photo opportunities with the poor but have little concern about producing measurable results. Price subsidies for goods and services for poor people just about always end up making things worse.

Even food given to people who are starving can cause problems. In 1981 IDE helped blacksmiths in refugee camps in Somalia build five hundred donkey carts and sell them for the local equivalent of four hundred fifty dollars on credit to other refugees, who promptly began to earn two hundred dollars a month after expenses by transporting water, firewood, and food. Whenever donated food was handed out, it was the highlight of the day in the camps. One of the items in the distributed food basket was powdered milk. I watched many refugees slit open bags of powdered milk and feed it to the goats. They had no use for it, but they loved camel's milk. Apparently nobody in the relief community had bothered to ask refugees if they would add water to powdered milk and drink it. On the other hand, cooking oil sold at a premium in the refugee marketplace, and so did the plastic jug it came in, because it was perfect as a water carrier.

Since an average donkey cart earned a net income of two hundred dollars a month, it could pay for itself in two-and-a-half months, including interest. So we proposed to UNHCR (United Nations High Commissioner for Refugees) that we provide the carts to refugees with 30 percent down and the rest on credit. We were met with outrage. UN refugee programs were equipped only to give things away. One UN official asked me indignantly what would happen if the money paid back by refugees were to be stolen by corrupt money managers. I replied that if it circulated two or three times and then was stolen, it would do two or three times as much good as circulating just once. I finally prevailed, but barely. After we repossessed two carts for nonpayment, we didn't have a single loan failure, and donkey cart owners became instant millionaires in the context of Somalia, because their net income of two hundred dollars a month was about fifteen times the income of the average person there.

Before I get totally carried away by my aversion to subsidies, I want to make it clear that there are areas such as education, roads, and health services that require public investment, and so does the creation of new markets in poor rural areas. That said, I believe the first step in finding a solution to just about any problem is to find ways to unleash market forces to solve it. If there is one thing I believe has created more obstacles to ending poverty than subsidies, it's the commonly held notion that you can donate people out of poverty.

To move out of poverty, poor people have to invest their own time and money. The path out of poverty lies in releasing the energy of Third World entrepreneurs. The good news is that the small-acreage farmers who make up the majority of dollar-a-day people are already entrepreneurs, and they are surrounded by thousands of other small-scale entrepreneurs operating workshops, stores, and repair shops. All these entrepreneurs are willing and able to invest in creating their own wealth if they can gain access to opportunities that are affordable and profitable enough to attract them.

In the first twenty years of my work with IDE, development leaders were outraged by my notion that you can and should sell things to poor people at a fair market price instead of giving things to them for nothing. "Business" was a dirty word to development organizations.

"It's exactly the multinational corporations that use the business approach you advocate who have caused the problem of poverty in the first place," they would say. "Poor people simply can't afford to buy the things they need, and they need these things very badly. The only way to make a real difference is to donate these things to them."

And the development organizations continued to donate mountains of food, free village hand pumps that broke down within a year and were never fixed, and thousands of free tractors that continue to rust under the African sun.

I'm happy to say that all this is now changing. With the abject failure of central planning in socialist countries, there is a new awareness in development circles that unleashing the energy of the marketplace is the best help we can give to poor people in their efforts to escape poverty permanently. Now people in the development field regard IDE's success in selling treadle pumps to 1.5 million poor farmers in Bangladesh as a pioneering piece of work. Suddenly leaders in irrigation, agriculture, economics, and design are keenly interested in what I have to say and I have more invitations to give keynote talks than I can handle.

Most importantly, more and more people are beginning to realize that making it possible for very poor people to invest their own time and money in attractive, affordable opportunities to increase their income is the only realistic path out of poverty for most of them.

NATIONAL ECONOMIC GROWTH WILL END POVERTY

The second myth is that poverty will be carried away on the coattails of national per capita economic growth. Two hundred and fifty years ago, 80 percent of the people in the world were just as poor as the 1.1 billion people today who survive on less than a dollar a day. Then the steam engine came along, and coal power, and the market forces that created the industrial revolution. This triggered two hundred and fifty years of successive waves of economic growth that eradicated the poverty of the great majority of the people in the world. Accordingly, we may fall prey to a second myth: all we need to do is maintain a consistently high per capita gross domestic product (GDP) in developing countries, and dollar-a-day poverty will end.

But in the United States, one of the richest countries in the world with persistent national economic growth over many generations, the US Census Bureau reported in 2005 that 37 million people, 12.6 percent of its total population, remained poor. India has sustained economic growth of 6 percent a year for many years, but in 1999 36 percent of its population, some 360 million people, still survived on less than a dollar a day. China has had an even more impressive sustained per capita GDP growth rate of 8 percent, and 16.6 percent of its 1.3 billion population, a total of 216 million people, were surviving on less than a dollar a day in 2001.[15] If sustained economic growth does end poverty, how is it that India and China, two developing countries with admirable sustained growth rates, still have some 575 million people who live in extreme poverty, most of whom also experience hunger?

It is because most of the poor people in the world live in remote rural areas that will likely continue to be bypassed by successive waves of urban-centered industrial growth. Industrial growth in urban areas leads national per capita GDP growth, and it generally bypasses the three-quarters of the dollar-a-day people who live in isolated rural areas and earn their living from tiny farms. Of course, many people who can't make it in rural areas migrate to cities to look for work, and some of them find it. Many end up in slums, and most quickly move back to their village if attractive jobs become available there.

It's true that we need growth to end poverty. But it is economic growth in remote rural areas on one-acre farms where poor people live that we need, not generic per capita GDP growth that takes place primarily through industrialization in urban areas. Ending urban poverty requires economic growth in slum areas, stimulated by creating new markets for informal slum-based enterprises that provide the jobs that poor people come to slums to get. This book will describe many new ways for poor farmers to increase the income they can earn from one-acre farms, and new ways for slum enterprises that employ poor people to increase their profitability.

Unless we can create economic growth and prosperity in the specific context of small, remote rural farms and of urban slums, the industrial growth that creates national GDP per capita growth will continue to bypass most poor people.

BIG BUSINESS WILL END POVERTY

Some people see a sickle as a weapon to start a revolution, others as a tool to bring in the harvest. But it is inherently neither of these. It is a curved piece of metal with a sharp edge and a wooden handle.

When I started IDE twenty-five years ago, poverty workers saw multinational corporations as evil oppressors of the poor, and business as the enemy. Now many see them as white knights ready to slay the poverty dragon. But a multinational corporation is inherently neither of these. It is an organizational structure for doing business. If most multinationals continue to operate the way they do now, the belief that big business will end poverty will remain nothing more than a tantalizing myth.

It is tantalizing because there are good reasons to think of big businesses as instruments to end poverty. If it's a fact that poor people need to increase their income, who knows more about how to make money than multinationals? But very few multinationals know how to make a profit serving customers who survive on less than a dollar a day, who may be illiterate, and who have no access to mass media. An increasing number of businesses are learning how to serve customers who earn four or five dollars a day, but in the context of most developing countries, these people belong to the middle class. To make an impact on poverty, big business has to learn how to provide affordable goods and services capable of increasing the income of very poor people, do it in volume, and make a profit doing it.

With his book *The Fortune at the Bottom of the Pyramid*, C.K. Prahalad has become a champion of the increasingly popular trend that sees existing multinationals taking action to end poverty.

"We start with a simple proposition," he says. "If we stop thinking of the poor as victims or as a burden and start thinking of them as resilient and creative entrepreneurs and value-conscious consumers, a whole new world of opportunity will open up."[16]

I couldn't agree more.

But the practical methods Prahalad proposes in order to take advantage of this new world of opportunity fall far short of the exciting vision he begins with. Like Jeff Sachs, he makes little attempt to set priorities for poverty alleviation initiatives, and treats with equal admiration all nine of the businesses he presents as exemplary models for poverty eradication. Most of them do, indeed, implement admirable programs. But they vary widely in their profitability and their impacts on poor people, and Prahalad, a professor in the University of Michigan Business School, provides no comparative analysis of the bottom-line profitability of the business performance of these companies or of the direct measurable impact of their activities on the lives of poor people.

Of the nine exemplary organizations he describes, one is not a business at all, but an admirable charity, three serve middle-class or richer customers, one provides useful epidemiological information but no data are available on its performance as a business, and four are engaged in activities that have differing financial performance and impacts on poor people.

Bhagwan Mahaveer Viklang Sahayata Samiti (BMVSS) is an admirable Indian nonprofit organization that provides the remarkable thirty-dollar Jaipur prosthetic foot to poor people in developing countries at no cost. But BMVSS is a charitable organization, not a business. Cemex has an excellent business model for marketing and providing credit for building supplies, and Casas Bahia provides similar excellence to customers for household appliances such as TV sets and refrigerators. Both of these companies serve middle-class customers who earn at least five or six dollars a day, not dollar-a-day people. The same is likely true for Annapurna Iodized Salt, whose product helps prevent iodine-deficiency illnesses, but it sells at a higher price than most very poor people can afford to pay. Voxiva provides an excellent model for obtaining mass information on population health that is particularly relevant for rapid response to epidemics. It is incorporated as a business but appears to operate more like an NGO executing grants, and since neither Prahalad nor Voxiva's Web site provides any information on Voxiva's financial performance, it is impossible to evaluate its performance as a business.

Four of the case studies Prahalad describes contain potentially useful examples for business opportunities that serve the poor. ICICI Bank, one of India's largest banks, provides a cost-effective model for forming more than eight thousand self-help groups (SHGs) of women who participate in the bank's savings and loan programs. Since these groups are organized by promoters who are SHG members paid on the basis of performance, this model appears to be a cost-effective way of scaling up the basic Grameen Bank approach. Unfortunately, it is not likely to be economically viable, although no profit/loss data are given. By providing timely market price information through Internet information centers, the e-Choupal system operating as a division of ITC, a large Indian company, increases the income of poor farmers by allowing them to sell at higher prices and receive information on improving their farming practices. No data on bottom-line profitability of this model are provided. Hindustan Lever, the Indian subsidiary of Unilever, launched a large-scale marketing initiative for its popular Lifebuoy brand of soap, which incorporated effective communication about the health benefits of hand washing, increasing its sales of

Lifebuoy by 30 percent and likely reducing the incidence of diarrhea and other illnesses among the rural poor. The Aravind Eye Care System uses profits earned from cataract operations performed for patients from the United Kingdom and those who can afford to pay in India, to provide the same service to patients who are too poor to pay.

Aravind provides cataract operations and the insertion of intraocular lenses for between $84 and $331, one-tenth of the cost for the same procedure in the United States. Between 1997 and 2002, Aravind carried out more than a million surgeries, a majority for poor people whose care was paid for with profits from patients with the ability to pay.[17] Data provided on both the financial performance of Aravind and its impact on the poor suggest that this is a good business model with positive impact on the poor, although probably less than one half of 1 percent of dollar-a-day people can benefit from affordable eye surgery.

To operate as a business rather than a charity, the Jaipur foot organization would need to create a strategy such as selling a two-thousand-dollar version of its foot to Western customers too poor to afford the eight-thousand-dollar model and using the profits to pay for and scale up the subsidized services it provides to poor customers.

Unfortunately, Prahalad places the 4 billion people in the world who earn one, two, three, and four dollars a day all in the same boat at the bottom of the pyramid. Then he cites exemplary businesses—such as Casas Bahia in Brazil and Cemex in Mexico, which serve middle-class customers—as models for the role big business can play in ending poverty. This is a bit like lumping together homeless people, people on welfare, social workers, schoolteachers, and nurses in the United States into one group at the bottom of the pyramid and citing a successful chain of Hyundai car dealers as an exemplary model for serving people at the bottom of the pyramid.

Big business certainly has the potential to make a huge positive impact on ending poverty and to earn good profits by doing it. To take advantage of this remarkable opportunity, multinationals must learn to think and operate in totally different ways. They will need to make radical changes in how they design, price, and deliver products and services to poor people. These radically different economically sustainable business models for making positive impacts on the lives of very poor people will need to incorporate the basic principles below.

1. First priority goes to models that effectively serve customers who live on less than a dollar a day.

2. Products and services are designed to reach price points affordable to people who earn less than a dollar a day, when sold at an unsubsidized fair market price.

3. First priority goes to the design and marketplace delivery of income-generating tools and strategies capable of at least paying for themselves in the first year.

4. The business model expressed in a viable business plan will be capable of reaching bottom-line profitability within a time frame acceptable to investors who fund the business.

5. Measurable positive impacts on poverty are an essential component of a viable business plan.

6. Capacity for scaling up the business to reach millions of poor customers is an essential component of a viable business plan.

Just as in the process by which the iPod evolved from the five-dollar transistor radio, designing and delivering products and services that are affordable enough to be attractive to dollar-a-day customers almost always leads to major market breakthroughs for wealthier customers. The experience of IDE and other organizations, such as KickStart, indicates that there are many products capable of earning a net return of 300 percent per year or more on the investment made to buy them by extremely poor customers. As their incomes increase from a dollar a day to three dollars a day and more, poor people become customers for a range of consumer goods, providing significant business opportunities for companies that have already attracted them as customers.

People who survive on less than a dollar a day have the lowest labor rates in the world — about one sixtieth of the minimum wage rate in the United States. In a global economy where the typing of medical records in American and European hospitals is outsourced to India and designer jeans sold in Europe are produced in China, the challenge for big business is to find ways to harness the five-cent-an-hour labor rates of dollar-a-day people and make a profit doing it. There already are successful models for doing this.

The Gujarat Cooperative Milk Marketing Federation (GCMMF) has grown rapidly to become India's largest food-products marketing organization. In 2005–2006, its sales turnover was $850 million handling 9.91 million liters of milk a day from 2.5 million small-farm milk producers, most of whom started out earning less than a dollar a day. Also known as Amul, this creative organization found a way to collect milk from farmers with one to three buffaloes, cool it, and process it into products such as fresh milk, butter, cheese, and ice cream, sold to people who can afford to buy them. There are 800 million dollar-a-day rural people, just like the small-acreage farmers who are member producers of Amul, who can harness their radically low labor costs to produce labor-intensive high-cost off-season fruits and vegetables, herbs, and the key essential oil ingredients for luxury cosmetics and Chanel No. 5 perfume, if big business can find ways of collecting them and marketing them to high-end markets as Amul does.

IDE, the organization that I founded, has already sold more than 2 million treadle pumps to dollar-a-day farm families, increasing their net annual income by more than 200 million dollars a year and creating a multiplier impact on poor villages of at least $500 million a year. Early market demand suggests that the global demand for low-cost drip systems will reach at least 10 million families, increasing their net annual income by $2 billion a year.

While the approaches of current development experts are dominated by myths such as the belief that we can donate people out of poverty, dollar-a-day families themselves have clear views about the main reason for their continued poverty-insufficient income. They also have clear ideas about what can be done to increase their income. By adopting their views, IDE has encouraged small-acreage farmers to invest in diversified, high-value, labor-intensive cash crops such as a variety of fruits, vegetables, and herbs. Stimulating the emergence of private-sector supply chains has provided access to affordable irrigation, seeds, and fertilizers. IDE, TechnoServe, and many other organizations have stimulated access to markets where one-acre farmers can sell their crops through private-sector value chains. By applying these principles,

IDE has been able to help between 2.5 million and 3 million dollar-a-day families to increase their net annual income significantly. Each of these families made considerable investments of their own time and money to move out of poverty.

Total investments by IDE and its donors in initiatives to end rural poverty over the past twenty-five years were $78 million. During the same time period, dollar-a-day farmers invested a total of $139 million in income-generating tools promoted by IDE. Their investments generated $288 million per year in permanent new net income. Taken over seven years, the net return to dollar-a-day small-acreage farmers is more than $2 billion (US) on a total investment by both IDE and its small-farm customers of $217 million. There is a clear pattern for most farmers to increase steadily both their investments in high-value farming and the net income they earn from it over time.

This is only a drop in the bucket in the context of 1.1 billion dollar-a-day people in the world. The good news is that potentially this approach can be scaled up to move 500 million or more rural dollar-a-day people out of poverty.

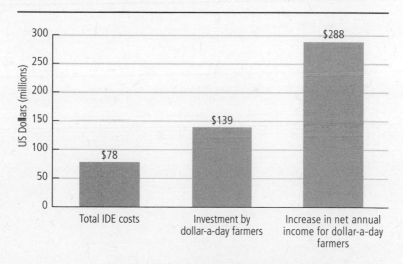

Table 2: IDE's Impact over Twenty-five Years

It is clear that without a revolution in thinking and practice on the part of the development community, the business community, and poor people themselves, we will never be able to end poverty. But if we learn to listen to poor people, understand the specific contexts in which they live and operate, and find ways to harness their entrepreneurial energy to increase their income, I have no doubt that at least 500 million families now surviving on less than a dollar a day will find practical ways to end their poverty within one generation.

Paul Polak, Bob Hyde, and a small-acreage farmer in India with his treadle pump

Small-acreage farmer proudly shows his drip-irrigated cucumbers.

CHAPTER THREE

It All Starts with Making More Money

AFTER KRISHNA BAHADUR THAPA AND I HAD COME TO KNOW
and trust each other a bit as we talked nonstop and walked together
through the scattered quarter-acre plots of his two-acre farm in Ekle
Phant village, I asked him a question.

"Bahadur, why are you poor, and what could you do to stop being
poor?"

He smiled shyly and his eyes crinkled, as if he were too polite to call
me an idiot to my face or to ask me if by any chance I might be blind.

"I'm poor because I haven't found a way to earn more money," he
said.

"Of course, my family and I are very lucky compared with some of
our neighbors. We have two acres of pretty good land, and we can produce enough rice to keep us from going hungry two years out of three.
We earn another twenty-five hundred rupees ($35 US) from selling
rainy-season vegetables and some black gram, and sometimes some
surplus rice, and my son Deu Bahadur and I can earn another five

thousand rupees or so from jobs in Mugling. Sometimes we take the bus to look for work in Kathmandu. But that isn't really enough to live on.

"We are poor because we can't earn a decent living from our farm, and it's hard to find work. When we do find work, it doesn't last long and doesn't pay enough to live on. Without our land, I don't know how we could survive.

"If we could only figure out a way to earn more money from my farm, we would stop being poor very quickly."

During the last twenty-five years, I've talked with more than three thousand poor families all over the world—families like Bahadur's—and they all tell me the same thing: the single most important thing they need to get out of poverty is to find a way to earn more money. This is so obvious that people tell me that it is a perfect example of circular logic. But the sad fact is that it isn't at all obvious to the great majority of the world's poverty experts.

"Poor people are poor because they have no power," says one influential group. "They are victims of a corrupt political system that maintains its own power by keeping poor people powerless. Find ways to empower the poor, give them a voice, give them entry to power in the political system that controls their lives, and their poverty will disappear."

"Poor people are locked into poverty because they are uneducated," says a second group. "How can you be expected to gain power over your life, or to know how to make anything happen, if you can't even read or write, much less qualify for a decent job? A good education is a human right," they say.

"Provide the children of very poor families with a decent education, and within the first generation, they will stop being poor. At the very least, they will qualify for decent jobs."

"None of these things will help if you come down with a bad case of malaria once a month that keeps you from working," a third group says. "If you live in Zambia or Zimbabwe today, you stand a pretty good chance of being an orphan by the time you are twelve because both of your parents will be dead from HIV/AIDS.

"The most effective way to end poverty is to eradicate major illnesses like polio, malaria, tuberculosis, and HIV/AIDS which cripple poor people and ensure that they stay poor. We must put in place programs to keep people healthy."

"You are all wrong!" says still another group of poverty experts. "The fact is that all these things are critically important. If you only fix education and ignore health, you're not that much better off. What good does it do if a poor person has a good education and then is crippled by malaria before he is twenty? Addressing one key factor—like transport or agriculture, or irrigation or drinking water or health—does no good unless you fix the problems in all the other key areas at the same time. It will cost a lot of money. But it's the only way to end poverty once and for all.

"Poor health, poor education, and lack of access to water and sanitation, and the other root causes of poverty all have to be addressed effectively at the same time to have any hope of ending poverty."

So now who are we to believe—poor people themselves, like Bahadur and his family, or most of the world's poverty experts?

On the face of it, the notion that poor people are poor because they don't have enough money seems hard to challenge. It's obvious if you talk to poor people and listen to what they have to say.

But it isn't so obvious if you start thinking too hard about it.

Listen, for instance, to what professors Paul Hunt, Manfred Nowak, and Siddiq Osmani have to say in a UN publication on poverty and human rights.

"There is an emerging view that poverty constitutes a denial or non-fulfillment of human rights. But does this mean that poverty is the same thing as non-fulfillment of human rights in general—i.e., does the non-fulfillment of any kind of human rights constitute poverty? Or should only certain kinds of human rights matter in the context of poverty? If so, how are we to decide which ones, and can the discourse on poverty be indifferent to the rest? These are the kinds of questions that need to be addressed."[18]

And these are the kinds of discussions that go on in the poverty field.

How on earth did things get so complicated?

A little bit of history might help explain it. The idea that rich countries could help poor countries move out of poverty has its roots in the dramatic success of the Marshall Plan in restoring the economies of Europe after World War II. In fact, the World Bank was then known as the Bank for Reconstruction and Development. But when the Bank tried to apply Marshall Plan–type strategies to the economies of very poor countries, they failed miserably. One of the reasons put forward for the failure was that poverty was too complex to be solved with economic strategies alone, and efforts to increase the income of poor people began to be regarded as hopelessly simplistic.

The Integrated Rural Development movement in the 1980s, for example, asserted that any effort to address only a single contributor to poverty is destined to fail. Since poverty is multidimensional, initiatives to end poverty had to address all of the key root causes of poverty simultaneously to be effective. I thought this was quite silly, and wrote a paper called "Segregated Rural Development" to which no one paid any attention. Not surprisingly, it proved to be just about impossible for any single organization to implement effective initiatives in health, education, transport, drinking water, housing, agriculture, women's rights, and food security all at the same time, so the Integrated Rural Development movement failed.

Of course, most major problems are complex, and if you want to understand a complex problem, you have to reach a thorough understanding of each of its root causes and how they interact. But finding a practical solution requires a different strategy. It is more a matter of finding the simplest single "lever" capable of producing the biggest positive result.

Malaria is a perfect example of a complex problem. It has a complex life cycle in its human and anopheles mosquito hosts, and a complex process governing the evolution of strains resistant to antimalaria medication, all factors that are profoundly influenced by changes in the environments of both the mosquito and the human parasite hosts. Yet a single, relatively simple, low-cost intervention can lower the incidence and prevalence of malaria — the widespread introduction of affordable insecticide-impregnated mosquito bed nets.

In spite of the complexity of the disease, the introduction of a simple barrier that prevents infected anopheles mosquitoes from injecting malaria parasites into the bloodstreams of people can stop the spread of malaria infection in its tracks. And if there are fewer people around carrying malaria parasites, fewer mosquitoes get infected by biting them. So malaria rates eventually go down, even for people without mosquito nets.

Such simple but critical high-leverage interventions can generate significant positive impacts on multiple fronts. I hear very few people complaining that the distribution of mosquito bed nets is a ridiculously simplistic approach to the complex problem of malaria, or that the use of penicillin is a ridiculously simplistic approach to the complex problem of pneumococcal pneumonia. Yet many leaders in development continue to scorn the search for relatively simple, low-cost, high-leverage solutions to the complex problem of poverty.

I have no doubt that the most important low-cost, high-leverage solution to the complex issue of poverty is helping poor people increase their income. Does this mean that increasing the income of poor people solves all the complex root causes of poverty by itself? Certainly not. And what impact would it have, if any, on education, health, agriculture, and the other root causes of poverty? The best way to answer this question is to let poor people who have increased their income speak for themselves.

I met John Mbingwe in an isolated rural village in Zambia in 2001. A lanky man in overalls, he walked us at a leisurely pace from the potholed dirt road past yellow-leaved stands of rain-fed maize to the one-acre plot of vegetables he grew for the Livingston market twenty-five kilometers away. For years, he had been growing vegetables by carrying water in buckets from the crude five-foot-deep well he and his wife had dug with a spade in the marshy part of his land called a *dambo*. But carrying water by bucket is very hard work, and he and his wife worked long hours to irrigate an eighth of an acre of vegetables. Then they borrowed enough money to install a treadle pump that they bought from a local dealer. With less labor than it took to water an eighth of an acre by bucket, he and his family suddenly found they could produce a full acre of vegetables. Within a year they had paid off the loan for the pump, increased their net annual income from three hundred to six hundred dollars, and they were on their way to earning more.

"What do you spend it on?" I asked.

"First of all, my wife and I are making sure our two sons have a good education," he said. "The government schools are free till grade six, but beyond that, we have to pay for school uniforms and books and some tuition, and that was just impossible for us before we increased our income. Before, we could barely afford buying clothes once a year for the boys, and buying school uniforms was out of the question, especially since we sometimes didn't even have enough to eat.

"Now we buy decent clothes, we put three meals on the table all year, and both boys will graduate from high school. My wife and I will have to do more of the work, but they can help us with the vegetables before they go to school and after school till it gets dark.

"We are thinking of investing in a used diesel pump so we can irrigate more land. And we are going to try growing paprika and maybe some marigolds next year. One problem is that we already have trouble doing the weeding and all the other work we have to do for a whole acre of vegetables.

"Does IDE have any labor-saving tools we can use?"

John's story is typical. Most poor people put a high priority on educating their kids. In countries like India and Bangladesh, where dowries are a fact of life, they educate their sons but not always their daughters. The most important investment for their daughters is to save for a dowry. It costs an average of a year's wages to provide a big enough dowry to attract a husband capable of providing for a daughter for the rest of her life.

Table 3 shows how one group of farmers in Nepal invested the new income they earned from growing off-season vegetables using IDE low-cost drip-irrigation systems.

What impact does increasing the income of poor people have on the powerlessness that so many poverty experts believe is the primary cause of poverty? Extremely poor families get their rights trampled on regularly. But what is the most direct path to power for powerless poor people? Increased income! Poor people don't usually talk much about power when I ask them how they invest their new income, but you can easily see the unobtrusive signs of their increased pride, assertiveness, and political influence.

In many rural areas, water is power. In poor villages where IDE worked in eastern India and Bangladesh, richer farmers with more land owned big, expensive wells that provided the only source of irrigation water. The local people called them "water lords," because with control of water, they could control the small-acreage poor farmers

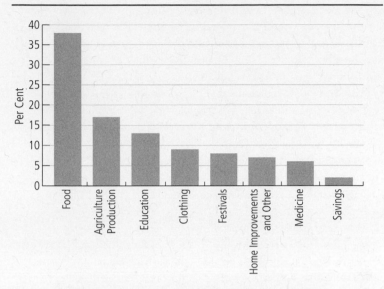

Table 3: How Small-Acreage Farmers in a Hill Village in Nepal
Invested the New Income They Earned from Growing Vegetables

whom they paid very low wages. But irrigation water was available twelve feet below the surface, and when we made eight-dollar treadle pumps available, small-acreage farmers gained access to their own source of irrigation water. The monopolistic power the water lords had over them was broken. The water lords still had paying jobs that small-acreage farmers needed, but now the poorer farmers could negotiate fair market wages.

What about housing?

When Abdul Rahman, a Bangladeshi farmer, started earning one hundred dollars a year in new income from growing and selling irrigated vegetables, one of the first things he and his family did was install a corrugated-tin roof. One September I was having tea with them in their small courtyard outside their two-room three-hundred-square-foot mud-and-wattle house. A little hut beside it served as a kitchen. Suddenly it began to rain hard, so we went inside. The rain on the corrugated tin roof sounded like sixteen machine gun batteries firing simultaneously, and all conversation stopped. But the thatched roof it replaced had leaked like a sieve, and under corrugated tin, the shiny clay/dung floor was dry. Not only that, but corrugated tin brought status and admiration from the neighbors.

Does increased income do anything for a poor family's health?

A thirty-year-old farmer in a remote rural area in Bihar had tears in his eyes when he told me about the serious illness his wife had come down with three years earlier.

"She coughed a lot—I think she had some kind of chest infection," he said. "I didn't have the money to buy medicines for her. She had a terrible fever, but after two days she seemed much better. Then she died in the middle of the night. I don't know what I would do if I didn't have my sister to help with my children."

If he had had a better income, this farmer could have taken his wife to a clinic or a local healer. The clinic might have been out of medicines and the local healer might or might not have been able to help, but if the clinic or the local folk healer had possessed the knowledge to assess his wife's illness and the right medicines to treat it, she might still be alive.

When people are too poor to pay for health services, they can only accept what the government or donors provide. When people have the capacity to pay, they are likely to choose and shape the health services that are important to them. The same freedom of choice goes for the schools where they send their children. Increased income provides more power and more choices.

But increased income improves family health in other ways as well.

Most poor people who survive on less than a dollar a day eat a very limited diet—a staple food such as rice, wheat, or corn, and different varieties of beans providing a balance of all the essential amino acids. A morsel of fish or meat might be added as a treat once a month, and fruits or vegetables are often pretty scarce. If they start to grow vegetables for the market, they always eat at least the ones that are over-ripe or have wormholes, and many families eat as much as half the vegetables they grow, even though they could make more money by selling them all instead. Fruits and vegetables, even the ones with wormholes, add vital minerals and vitamins to the diet of the poor. Some children in very poor rural families go blind from vitamin A deficiency, a condition that is preventable by eating yellow vegetables. Most dollar-a-day families go hungry for two or three months a year, which makes them much more vulnerable to disease. One of the first things they spend their new income on is buying the food they need to assuage their hunger.

Most very poor families have no access to clean water, so they drink water loaded with pathogens. They usually know that this gives their children diarrhea, which puts young children at risk of dying, but they have no choice. With a little extra income, they invest in a seven-dollar water filter or a low-cost hand pump. When IDE was able to halve the cost of installed hand pumps in Vietnam, national sales doubled. In most rural cultures, when a family installs a low-cost hand pump, the neighbors are welcome to use it too. A surprising number of poor rural families in Vietnam have now demonstrated that when the marketplace makes low-cost latrines available, these families are also willing and able to invest in ones that fit their preferences.

When a family increases its income, its members are likely to be healthier, get sick less often, and stay sick for shorter periods of time. Of course, this does not eliminate the need for publicly funded clinics and for initiatives to contain such serious illnesses as malaria, tuberculosis, and HIV/AIDS.

Does increasing the income of poor people make any difference for agriculture? For the rural poor, reinvestment in agriculture is a major opportunity to continue to increase income, so it is not surprising that a significant percentage of new income is reinvested in livestock or improved farming and, if there is a real windfall, in purchasing a little more land. Many invest in expanded irrigation or improved seeds and more fertilizer, so they can earn more from their next crop without having to wait for the government or donors to assist them.

Very poor people who live in urban slums rarely grow much, although sometimes they have access to small patches of land where they can grow cash crops. If they are lucky enough to land a job that pays well, they are more likely to invest some of their income in trading or in small-business opportunities than in growing things.

Do poor families invest much of their new income in improvements in energy? The most common energy source for poor people is their own backs. There are 8 million or more small-acreage farmers in Africa who use buckets to carry water to their crops from streams or ponds. They are quick to invest in more efficient ways to harness their own energy, devices such as treadle pumps or low-cost drip-irrigation systems that save energy by decreasing the amount of water that has to be lifted manually from a well.

Most dollar-a-day farmers cultivate with hoes. A tractor is a distant dream, and so is spending a hundred and fifty dollars for a draft animal. A few are able to pay for a neighbor to bring his bullock and plow to prepare their rice fields for planting.

Most very poor rural families have no access to electricity, and often pay two to five dollars a month for candles, kerosene for a lamp, and flashlight batteries. So they go to sleep when it gets dark, and they get up at dawn. Many urban slum dwellers get illegal access to electricity by throwing a wire over a power line, but that source is unavailable to the rural poor. With new sources of income, poor families in both urban and rural areas readily invest in affordable improved energy sources for their households, such as three-dollar rechargeable flashlights or twelve-dollar solar lanterns.

The variety of goods transported on people's backs in poor villages is astonishing. Most very poor people can only dream of owning a bicycle. When these people earn more money, many buy a used bicycle, which they use for hauling things more than for personal transport. But their most popular transport technology is that of using their own two feet. Poor people certainly use buses and rickshaws sometimes, because they are cheap. Donkeys, bullocks, and camels all are used to pull carts, but for most very poor people, all these animals are too expensive to buy. For some city slum dwellers, operating a rickshaw provides a source of income. But that rickshaw puller most likely leases the rickshaw from an owner of a rickshaw fleet.

It all boils down to this: While it certainly is true that powerlessness, poor health, poor education, and absent transport infrastructure are important root causes of poverty, there can be no question that the most direct and cost-effective first step out of poverty is to find ways to help poor people to increase their income. This allows them to make their own choices about which root causes of poverty to address. The most effective way to help poor people increase their income is to bring new life and profitability to the grassroots enterprises, such as small farms in rural areas and countless small businesses in urban slums, where poor people earn their livings.

Thatched-roof, dung-and-wattle house (India) with no market value and no collateral value

CHAPTER FOUR

Design for the Other 90 Percent

WHEN BAHADUR'S FAMILY, WITH THE HELP OF HELVETAS, gained access to a half-inch pipe full of water coming to their house, they saw right away that they could use it to water a few vegetables. They just held the pipe and let the water fall onto the plants. But they couldn't figure out how to use it to irrigate a whole field of vegetables. Of course, they had never heard of drip irrigation, and even if they had, the smallest available drip system would have cost two thousand dollars, far more than Bahadur's family could afford.

A world-class irrigation expert like Jack Keller probably could have given them three practical solutions to their problem in ten minutes, but there were no Jack Kellers available. Bahadur and his family had no knowledge of modern plastics, or they might have been able to design a usable low-cost drip system themselves. I learned about farmers in Thailand who designed their own low-cost drip system by letting water dribble out of discarded intravenous tubes they got from a hospital and inserted into plastic water lines. But without the help or information they needed, Bahadur's family was stuck. Small-acreage farmers like Bahadur have hundreds of critical problems like this that modern designers with access to worldwide information could solve rapidly.

The problem is that 90 percent of the world's designers spend all their time working on solutions to the problems of the richest 10 percent of the world's customers. A revolution in design is needed to reverse this silly ratio and reach the other 90 percent.

Transport engineers work to create elegant shapes for modern cars while most of the people in the world dream of being able to buy a used bicycle. As designers make products more stylish, efficient, and durable, prices go up, but people with money are able and willing to pay. In contrast, the poor in developing countries—who outnumber their rich, urban counterparts by twenty to one—have only pennies to spend on hundreds of critical necessities. They are ready to make any reasonable compromise in quality for the sake of affordability, but nothing is available in the marketplace to meet their needs.

The fact that the work of modern designers has almost no impact on most of the people in the world is not lost on those entering the design field. Bernard Amadei, an engineering professor at University of Colorado in Boulder, tells me that engineering students all over the United States and Canada are flocking to take advantage of opportunities made available by organizations such as Engineers Without Borders to work on problems such as designing and building affordable rural water-supply systems in poor countries.

If students can make meaningful contributions to design for poor customers, why does this area continue to be ignored? Is it because it is much more difficult than designing for the rich? I don't think so.

How Complicated Is It to Design for the Poor?

You don't need a degree in engineering or architecture to learn how to talk with and listen to poor people as customers. I've been doing it for twenty-five years. The things they need are so simple and so obvious that it is relatively easy to come up with new, income-generating products for which they are happy to pay. But these products have to be cheap enough to be affordable to the poor.

Twenty-three years ago in Somalia, International Development Enterprises undertook its first project by helping refugee blacksmiths build and sell five hundred donkey carts to fellow refugees. But there are a lot of thorns on the dirt roads in Somalia they traveled, and nowhere for a donkey cart owner to buy tools to fix flat tires. So I went to Nairobi and bought tube-patch kits; a large number of good-quality, twelve-dollar, British-made lug wrenches that carried a virtual lifetime guarantee; and a few six-dollar Chinese-made models that would be lucky to last six months. I offered both types of lug wrenches for sale to donkey cart owners at my cost.

To my amazement, the Chinese lug wrenches sold like hotcakes, while I failed to sell a single British model. How could this be? After talking to a lot of donkey cart owners, I realized a donkey cart operator could generate enough income in one month to buy ten British-made lug wrenches, but if he didn't have the money to buy a lug wrench to fix today's flat tire, he would earn nothing and might end up losing his donkey cart. So he bought the wrench he could afford in order to stay in business today and earn more money for tomorrow. Hundreds of poor people I talked to told me the same kind of story. For the 2.7 billion people in the world who earn less than two dollars a day, affordability rules.

The Ruthless Pursuit of Affordability

Vince Lombardi, famous coach of the Green Bay Packers, often said to his football players, "Winning isn't everything; it's the only thing."

With one word change, the same sentiment applies to the process of designing products to serve poor customers: "Affordability isn't everything. It's the only thing."

I have to confess that I am a born cheapskate, so the notion of putting affordability first comes naturally. When I need an umbrella, instead of buying a thirty-eight-dollar designer model in the department store, I opt for a functional black one bought for one dollar at the local Dollarama, where everything costs a dollar or less. I know the thirty-eight-dollar model will last a lot longer, but I also know that I will probably forget it somewhere within a month. If that one-dollar umbrella keeps my head dry for just one rain shower or, better still, for a couple of months before I lose it, I've saved myself thirty-seven dollars.

The rural poor think in much the same way, with one critical difference—they will keep that one-dollar umbrella in good working order for seven years, at the end of which it will have more patches on it than Jacob's coat and three or four improvised splints on the handle yet will still be usable far into the future.

There is another big difference. To earn a single dollar, an unskilled laborer in the United States needs only to work about ten minutes, while his counterpart in Bangladesh or Zimbabwe must work for two full days. The equivalent of a Dollarama in the developing world would be a Pennyrama. To learn how to come up with affordable products for poor customers in developing countries, Western designers would do well to start with a brainstorming exercise to develop a serviceable ten-cent umbrella. But designers in the industrialized world continue to design the equivalent of thirty-eight-dollar umbrellas for the world's rural poor.

How Many Ants Does It Take to Make a Horse?

Put yourself in the shoes of Peter Mukula, a poor farmer who lives along a dusty road twenty-five kilometers from Livingstone in southern Zambia. If he could afford to buy a packhorse, he could make an extra six hundred dollars a year hauling vegetables to the Livingstone market. But there's no way he can beg, borrow, or steal the five hundred dollars it would take to buy a horse today. Try this brainteaser—see if you can think of a practical solution to Peter's dilemma.

Let me throw out some crazy ideas. What if Peter could buy a quarter-horse? Not a purebred quarter horse, but a horse that's a quarter the size of a regular packhorse. Let's assume that he could buy such a miniature horse for one hundred and fifty dollars and that it could pack sixty kilograms. Peter would earn less money each trip, but he could gradually use his profits to buy more miniature horses. Once he owned four of them, they would be hauling the same two hundred and forty kilos as a full-size packhorse.

But even if a small packhorse were available, one hundred fifty dollars is still far more than what Peter could afford to pay. Perhaps he could find a pygmy horse one-twelfth the size of a standard horse that would cost fifty dollars and carry twenty kilos. After five years, Peter might be able to expand to a string of twelve pygmy horses and earn the six hundred dollars a year, the same as he would with a full-size packhorse. Interestingly enough, purebred miniature horses thirty-five inches high and weighing one hundred fifty to three hundred pounds are available. Unfortunately, they cost fifteen hundred to three thousand dollars!

Here's an even crazier idea. Suppose we could invent a way to harness the remarkable strength-to-weight ratio of the common forest ant? An engineering class in Germany designed tiny weights that could be attached to an ant's back and determined that forest ants can carry as much as thirty times their own weight. (A human can only carry about double.) How many ants would it take to carry the same load as a packhorse?

I did the numbers. It would take 1.25 million ants to carry Peter's two hundred forty kilos. Now 1.25 million ants would come pretty cheap. But designing the harness would be a challenge.

I have taken you through this imaginary design scenario to illustrate the central task of designing for poor customers—coming up with breakthroughs in both *miniaturization* and *affordability*, following exactly the same process as Henry Ford or Jobs and Wozniak. The next step in the holy trinity of affordable design is to make the new product *infinitely expandable*. If a farmer needs to drip-irrigate half an acre (two thousand square meters) but doesn't have enough cash to buy a half-acre drip system, he can buy a one-sixteenth-acre drip system and use the two hundred fifty dollars in net income it generates to expand to a half-acre system in the second year.

From Forest Ants to the Aswan Dam

Now, if you think the process of breaking a horse into twelve affordable pieces is complicated, try wrapping your mind around the problem of breaking down the Aswan Dam's water storage capacity into millions of ant-size pieces representing the small farms that could be nourished by the water stored in five-hundred-kilometer-long Lake

Nasser. Big dams such as Aswan are built to provide answers to the twin global problems of flooding and water scarcity. But when it comes to delivering irrigation water to poor, one-acre farms, giant dam water-storage systems are usually of little help.

The Nawsa Mad System

Spell Aswan Dam backward and you get "Nawsa Mad." This futuristic system would smooth out some of the peaks and valleys between perennial flooding and drought with the same strategy used by the Aswan Dam, but shrunk down to one four-millionth of its size so that it fits a two-acre farm and a small-acreage farmer's pocketbook. It is the ant to the Aswan Dam's horse.

In May 2003, I was interviewing farmers in Maharastra, India, who were using low-cost drip-irrigation systems to make the water in their open wells stretch a lot further than the flood irrigation they had been using. But the sixty-foot-deep, twenty-five-foot-diameter wells that were the only source of irrigation water during the dry season cost one hundred thousand rupees to build (about two thousand dollars US). Because the wells were so expensive, only 25 to 40 percent of the farmers in Maharastra owned one. The rest earned a paltry income from rain-fed farming and could survive only by finding work outside their farms.

But rainwater ran off their fields in sheets during the monsoon season in June, July, and August. What if we could find a cheap, simple way to trap some of this monsoon rainwater and store it until the dry season from March to May, when vegetable and fruit prices were at their peak, and deliver the water to crops through a low-cost drip-irrigation system?

To create a miniaturized, on-farm version of the Aswan Dam, we had to find ways to:

1. Collect monsoon rainwater on individual farms.

2. Settle out the silt and mud in it before storing it.

3. Store it for six months with no evaporation.

4. Deliver it from storage to crops without wasting a drop.

5. Most importantly, develop the whole system cheaply enough to be *affordable* to a poor farm family living on three hundred dollars a year, *profitable* enough to pay for itself in the first year, and *infinitely expandable* using the profits it generates.

Solutions for 1, 2, and 4 were easy. There were already all kinds of rainwater-harvesting systems in place that collected, settled, and stored rainwater, and the low-cost drip-irrigation system designed by IDE provided the means to deliver it efficiently to crops. The critical missing link was a zero-evaporation, enclosed water-storage system for individual farms that was cheap enough to pay for itself in the first growing season.

We estimated that a farmer could reasonably be expected to clear fifty dollars from drip-irrigated, high-value crops grown on a one hundred-square-meter plot in the dry season using ten thousand liters of stored water. So we set a retail price target of forty dollars for the ten-thousand-liter enclosed storage tank. This was a daunting target, since the cost of a ten-thousand-liter ferro-cement tank in India starts at two hundred fifty dollars. So we came up with the idea of a ten-meter-long, double-walled plastic sausage in an earth trench. By using the earth around it for structural support, we could reach our price objective of forty dollars for a ten-thousand-liter storage tank. This would allow farmers to harvest monsoon rainwater, store it for six months or so without evaporation losses, and then apply it through a low-cost drip system to dry-season crops that sell at two or three times their normal prices.

The Nawsa Mad concept makes use of three new, affordable, small-plot-irrigation technologies that small-acreage farmers have desperately needed for centuries—a very low-cost enclosed water-storage system into which they can direct monsoon rainwater, a low-cost efficient way of pumping water from storage to the field, and a low-cost drip system to deliver it efficiently to high-value dry-season crops. You can take the same elements and use them to create a two-hundred-thousand-liter pond, with a plastic liner and a floating lid, that costs four hundred dollars and stores enough water to drip-irrigate a quarter acre of dry-season fruits and vegetables that will earn five hundred dollars after expenses.

Here are some of the other critical, affordable small-farm irrigation tools that IDE and a few other organizations are designing, field-testing, and marketing.

- **Improved treadle pumps that are cheaper and pump deeper**
  Several multidisciplinary teams at the Stanford design school have created more affordable versions of treadle pumps for Myanmar, and KickStart has recently introduced a more afford-able version for Kenya called the hip pump.

- **Motorized rope-and-washer pumps for irrigation**
  Rope-and-washer pumps provide affordable water-lifting at depths beyond the range of the treadle pump. Because it is diffi-cult to use human power alone to lift the volumes of water re-quired for irrigation, rope-and-washer pumps combined with microdiesel engines have potential to irrigate high-value crops from deeper water sources.

- **Lower-cost wind and solar pumping systems**
  Photovoltaics and wind energy have been too expensive for small farms, but ways of concentrating solar energy and making more-affordable windmills hold promise for small-acreage farmers.

- **Improved low-cost well-drilling tools**
  Practica, a Dutch organization, and several other development organizations are working to make a variety of affordable drilling techniques available to small farms.

- **A range of affordable enclosed water-storage systems, with one-thousand- to three-hundred-thousand-liter capacity**
  These are the systems I have described in Chapter 6 on affordable irrigation for small farms, which also describes the development of the microdiesel engine.

- **A one-hundred-dollar quarter-hp microdiesel pump set**

- **Larger low-cost drip systems with pre-installed emitters**
  The dramatic drop in price for drip irrigation has made it profitable for small-acreage farmers to use drip systems on lower-value

crops such as cotton and sugar cane, and some of them are even irrigating alfalfa for their milk buffaloes. I believe that low-cost drip systems like those developed by IDE will, over the next ten years, take over the majority of the world market for drip irrigation.

* **Low-cost low-pressure sprinkler systems**
  Low-cost drip irrigation works well for crops planted in rows. For crops not planted in rows—like wheat, mustard, and clover—the low-pressure affordable sprinkler system developed by Jack Keller and IDE in India provides more-efficient water distribution than does the flooding method.

* **A low-cost small-plot piped-water surface-irrigation system**
  By using a system of thin-walled tubes to deliver water to hand-formed micro-reservoirs, Jack Keller and IDE India are working to develop an efficient, low-cost surface-water delivery system suitable for small plots.

These are some of the design challenges for affordable small-plot irrigation systems. A similar array of design challenges exist for small-farm planting, harvesting, and postharvest-processing tools. Below are some examples.

* **A fifteen-dollar scythe for harvesting rice, corn, and wheat**
  This may surprise you, but most of the small-acreage farmers in the world still use a sickle to harvest their plots of rice and wheat. This usually takes several days, and in some places delays planting the next crop enough that it is impossible to grow a third crop. Of course, in Europe, peasants progressed from sickles to scythes, and then to wooden-fingered scythes called "cradles," which bunched the grain at the same time it was being cut. These tools were replaced by horse-drawn reapers and, eventually, by modern combines. If we went back in history to find the most efficient device to harvest wheat or rice from the typical quarter-acre plots of dollar-a-day farmers, it would probably be the cradle. We have a range of modern inexpensive, stronger, lighter materials such as fiberglass that could be used to improve both the wooden handle

and the blade of the scythes and cradles used more than a hundred years ago. A fifteen-dollar cradle would dramatically improve the harvesting efficiency on millions of small farms.

• **Postharvest processing**
Small-acreage farmers need a range of new postharvest process-ing tools capable of adding value at the farm or the village level, parallel to the design and dissemination of affordable small-plot irrigation and harvesting tools. These include:

• **A fifteen-hundred-dollar and a five-thousand-dollar steam distil-lation unit for essential oils**
These units are described in Chapter 8.

• **A fifty-dollar gasifier for generating heat**
Many value-added processing procedures for crops produced on small farms require uniform heat. Silk reeling, for example, heats harvested cocoons in water to cause them to give up silk threads. A gasifier heats with a fuel source such as wood chips in the absence of air to produce burnable gases, acting some-what like propane, that can be directed to a burner, providing uniform heat. A two-thousand-dollar gasifier developed in India by the Tata Energy Research Institute, backed by the Swiss government, cut wood use in silk reeling operations by 50 per-cent and produced a greater percentage of first-grade silk. De-signing a commercial gasifier at the target price of fifty dollars would allow a variety of drying and other value-added process-ing procedures to be carried out at the village or farm level.

• **Low-cost solar dryers to dry tomatoes and banana chips for high-end markets**

These are typical examples—the need for affordable farm-based value-added processing tools is longer than the one for affordable small-plot irrigation.

There is an even longer list for a range of consumer goods that dol-lar-a-day people are eager to buy when they increase their income, and people who earn two to six dollars a day are ready to buy now. This in-cludes the billion or so people who would be customers for two-dollar eyeglasses if somebody would design an effective global distribution and marketing system for them (see Chapter 8). There are more than a billion people in the world who will never connect to the electric-power grid who would be interested in buying a ten-dollar solar lantern, made possible by advances in light-emitting diodes (LEDs). More than a billion people would be willing customers for a four-dollar household-level filter that would make water safe to drink.

An attractive hundred-dollar house would make a huge positive impact on the lives of poor rural people.

A Hundred-Dollar House

In light of the fact that most young people in North America and Europe now can't afford to buy a house, it is remarkable that most of the 800 million rural people in the world who earn less than a dollar a day own the home they live in. But if they tried to sell it, they would get no money for it, and if they tried to offer it as collateral for a loan from a local banker, they would get turned down. This is because their home, made of sticks and wattle, with a thatched roof and dung floor, has no value in the local market and they have no opportunity to build something with value at a price they can afford.

But in every village, there are a few families who have a house built out of brick or cement block, with a tile roof, and these houses have both sales value and collateral value. They accomplish this by building it twenty-five bricks at a time, whenever they have a bit of cash left over, and taking ten or twenty years to do it. They take so long because construction loans aren't available in most of these places. I have seen far too many designs from Western architects for refugee camp shelters that look elegant to the Western eye and start at nine hundred dollars, or dwellings for poor rural families for fifteen hundred dollars and up, prices that are far too high to be affordable for dollar-a-day people.

The no-value stick-and-thatch home lacks a stable foundation and structural skeleton that will last. All we need to start a salable, bankable, twenty-square-meter home is eight strong beams and a solid roof that doesn't leak. Initially, this durable structural skeleton can be filled in with local materials—for example, sticks chinked with mud for the walls. Then, as money becomes available, stick walls can be replaced with cement block or brick, twenty-five bricks at a time.

If, from the beginning, the one-hundred-dollar house is designed to accept added modules, in the manner of a LEGO set, the family who lives in it can eventually own a house as big as they can afford. When the bankable house is completed, the family has a source of collateral so they can borrow the money they need for inputs, implements, and livestock to increase the income they earn from farming.

A Revolution in Design

Designing products that are attractive to poor customers requires a revolution in the design process. This revolution is already happening. In the summer of 2007, Cooper-Hewitt Design Museum in New York, one of the Smithsonian museums, opened an exhibit called "Design for the Other 90 Percent,"[19] in which thirty-six examples of designs for the poor from all over the world are displayed. Included are several treadle pumps, a low-cost drip system, low-cost water purification systems, and a technology that allows village entrepreneurs to turn sugar cane leaves into marketable charcoal briquettes. The design community is fascinated with this exhibit, which has received ever-increasing press coverage.[20] More recently, we have incorporated an organization called D-Rev: Design for the Other Ninety Percent,[21] whose mission is to create the design revolution. My dream is to implement four initiatives at the same time:

1. Transform the way design is taught in developed countries, to embrace design for the other 90 percent of the world's population.

2. Transform the way design is taught in developing countries, to embrace design for the other 90 percent of the world's people.

3. Establish a platform for ten thousand or more of the world's best designers to develop practical solutions to the real-life problems of poor people.

4. Give birth to international for-profit companies that profitably mass-market to poor customers critical technologies such as two-dollar eyeglasses.

To be successful, the process of design for the other 90 percent needs to follow a set of principles and practical steps that depart radically from conventional design.

The Principles of Design for the Other 90 Percent

Miniaturization, the ruthless pursuit of affordability, and infinite expandability are the three building blocks necessary to "design cheap." Now here is some music to go with the lyrics.

THE POOR CUSTOMER RULES THE DESIGN PROCESS

Thinking of poor people as customers instead of as recipients of charity radically changes the design process. Poor persons won't invest in a product or service unless the designer knows enough about the preferences of poor people to create something they value. The process of affordable design starts by learning everything there is to learn about poor people as customers, along with what they are able and willing to pay for something that meets their needs. When in doubt, I resort to the "Don't bother" trilogy.

ADOPT THE "DON'T BOTHER" TRILOGY

1. If you haven't had good conversations, with your eyes open, with at least twenty-five poor people before you start designing, don't bother.

2. If what you design won't at least pay for itself in the first year, don't bother.

3. If you don't think you can sell at least a million units at an unsubsidized price to poor customers after the design process is completed, don't bother.

SMALL IS STILL BEAUTIFUL

E.F. Schumacher was right on target by writing beautifully about smallness, even though he didn't focus enough on affordability and marketability. A modern combine doesn't even have room to turn around on a typical quarter-acre plot of a small-acreage farmer, much less harvest the plot. Seventy-five percent of all farms in Bangladesh and India are less than five acres, and in China less than half an acre. Since most of these small farms are further divided into several quarter-acre plots, this is the gauge against which any new technology for small-plot farmers must be evaluated.

For those trying to survive on a one-acre farm, a pinch of seed is better than a bagful. For a long time economists have talked about the "divisibility" of technology. You can't take a tractor and cut it up into little pieces, so economists give it the rather curious but descriptive label of "lumpy input." But a twenty-kilo bag of carrot seeds can be easily divided into packets just the right size to plant two rows in a kitchen garden.

Doing the same thing with mechanical technologies such as irrigation, tilling, and harvesting devices as can be done with a bag of seeds is probably the most important challenge in designing cheap. A center-pivot sprinkler system is very efficient, costs a ton of money, and is designed to fit a one-hundred-and-sixty-acre field. How do we design a low-pressure sprinkler system that distributes water just about as efficiently as a center-pivot system, costs less than twenty-five dollars, and works on a quarter-acre field? An Israeli drip-irrigation system is very efficient, costs a ton of money, and is designed to fit fields larger than five acres. How do we design a drip-irrigation system that is just about as efficient as the Israeli system, costs less than twenty-five dollars, and fits perfectly into a quarter-acre plot? IDE has made great strides in solving both these design problems, but there are thousands more like them that have yet to be addressed.

CHEAP IS BEAUTIFUL TOO

Shrinking a drip-irrigation system from ten acres to a quarter acre not only makes it appropriate for a poor farmer's small field, but also makes it considerably cheaper. In India, a two-cigarette package probably costs more per cigarette than the normal twenty-cigarette package, but it brings the purchase price down to an affordable level for a customer without much money. Affordability is the most important consideration in providing small-acreage farmers with access to income-generating technologies. Below are some guidelines I've found for designing cheap.

1. **Put tools on a radical weight-loss diet.** You can cut the cost if you can find a way to cut the weight. A good example of this is a small drip-irrigation system where most of the weight is in the plastic pipes. We cut the weight and the price of pipe by cutting system pressure by 80 percent. Doing this allowed us also to cut the wall thickness and weight of the plastic by 80 percent with a corresponding drop in price.

2. **Make redundancy redundant.** If a western engineer is asked to design a bridge capable of holding a ten-ton load, he is likely to build it to hold a thirty-ton load to lower the risk of a lawsuit if the bridge collapses. Because the legal risks are so much lower in poor countries, and affordability is so much more important, an engineer designing a water pipe for ten-pounds-per-square-inch pressure has no need to make the walls thick enough to withstand thirty-pounds-per-square-inch pressure. Eleven- or twelve-pounds-per-square-inch standard is sufficient.

3. **Move forward by designing backward.** Often, the most effective way to optimize affordability is to go back through the history that led to the modern form of the technology.

4. **Jazz up the old package with cutting-edge materials.** Update outmoded designs with any new materials that may have become available. As long as affordability is not compromised, all's fair.

5. **Make it as infinitely expandable as a LEGO set.** After miniaturization and affordability, infinite expandability is the third pillar of designing cheap. Initially, if a farmer can afford a drip system that irrigates only a sixteenth of an acre, design it so he can use the income it generates to double or triple its size the next year.

Practical Steps for Design for the Other 90 Percent

Here are some basic steps that I've found can cut the price of almost any expensive technology or tool by at least 50 percent.

SET A SPECIFIC PRICE TARGET

To be successful, the product or service you design has to meet a specific price point that poor customers are willing and able to pay. I usually start by setting a retail target price point that is about one-fifth of the price a product is selling for now. Since the price of ferro-cement water tanks in India starts at one rupee/liter, we set a target price for the design of an affordable water-storage unit at one-fifth rupee/liter.

ANALYZE WHAT THE TECHNOLOGY DOES

Make a list of the important functions that the technology will perform for the poor customers who will buy it.

IDENTIFY THE KEY CONTRIBUTORS TO COST

Identifying the key contributors to the cost of the current technology, from most to least important, provides a road map to finding affordable alternatives acceptable to poor customers. A key contributor to the cost of sprinkler systems is the thickness of the wall of the plastic lines carrying water to the sprinklers. Lowering the pressure in the system made it possible to use thinner-walled tubing.

DESIGN AROUND EACH OF THE KEY CONTRIBUTORS TO COST BY FINDING ACCEPTABLE TRADE-OFFS

Selecting acceptable trade-offs requires an intimate knowledge of the customer's situation and needs. Conventional drip-irrigation systems require a significant investment in a high-quality filter to prevent clogging of drip emitters. An alternative that small-acreage farmers find easily acceptable is to replace the expensive filter with a low-cost wire-mesh filter covered with a piece of cloth. The farmer's children can wash the cloth regularly and unplug clogged holes with a safety pin.

The key affordability trade-offs are:

1. **Capital for labor.** Since most poor people in rural areas are long on labor and short on cash, they will jump at almost any opportunity to trade capital cost for labor. Because of its lower cost, some farmers prefer to buy a smaller drip-irrigation system and shift it from row to row. Truckers in Nepal rarely invest in preventive maintenance — it's usually cheaper to wait till a part breaks, and then spend a few hours on the side of the road fixing it.

2. **Quality vs. affordability.** In the West, customers expect a tool to last at least seven years. Because of the lower cost, small-farm customers for treadle pumps or drip systems usually prefer a two-year product to a seven-year one. Always short of cash, they can use the 300 percent net annual return of a treadle pump to buy a seven-year pump if they want to after the first two years are up.

MAKE A MULTITUDE OF PROTOTYPES

The rapid prototyping process that is standard practice for design firms like IDEO fits perfectly for design for the poor. Using local rural workshops to produce prototypes is an advantage because they incorporate solutions to the constraints in materials and fabrication for the eventual local manufacture of the technology.

MAKE CHANGES BASED ON FIELD TESTS

Immediately after the proof-of-concept prototype stage, try out the new technology on at least twenty small farms with different conditions. Next, thoroughly question the farmers about what worked and what didn't, and then modify the technology based on their experiences.

ADAPT A TECHNOLOGY IF YOU MOVE IT TO A NEW PLACE

Bad news: Like fine wines, many technologies don't travel well. The good news is that the adaptation problems are usually easy to fix. That is why it never ceases to amaze me that anyone would consider exporting tractors from the United States to Africa, or low-cost drip-irrigation systems from India to China, without first going through the relatively inexpensive process of field-testing and adaptation based on experience.

Many people tell me that designers don't work on solving the problems of 90 percent of the world's customers because there is no money to be made doing it. I see this as only a temporary aberration.

That's Where the Money Will Be

I keep asking why 90 percent of the world's designers work exclusively on products for the richest 10 percent of the world's customers. Willie Sutton, the infamous bank robber, was once asked why he robbed banks.

"Because that's where the money is," he said.

I suspect my question about the world's designers has exactly the same answer.

I have no problem with people who make money by designing products for the rich. My friend Mike Keiser, with no more professional training than his love of golf and nature, designed a golf course and resort—Bandon Dunes, on a spectacular section of Oregon coastline—that quickly became the number-two golf destination in America. Such entrepreneurial brilliance deserves to be rewarded.

What astonishes me is that the huge, unexploited market that includes billions of poor customers continues to be ignored by designers and the companies for which they work. In this, however, they are following a well-established tradition.

If you had asked a car manufacturer before Henry Ford came along why he designed only big, expensive, custom cars for playboys, I suspect his answer would be the same as Willie Sutton's: "Because that's where the money is."

But it's not where the money is now.

Before Steve Jobs and Steve Wozniak came along with the personal computer, if you had asked the CEO of IBM why his company built only computers that cost $2 million and filled entire rooms, he would undoubtedly have said, "Because that's where the money is."

But, again, it's not where the money is now.

Before the advent of transistor radios and Walkmans, had you asked the executives of RCA why they made only hi-fi systems that cost thousands of dollars, they would also have given Willie Sutton's answer: "Because that's where the money is."

But it's not where the money is now.

Today, you could ask the executives of Netafim, the world's biggest drip-irrigation company, why more than 95 percent of their products go to the richest 5 percent of the world's farmers, and they would say, "Because that's where the money is."

But think about this. If 100 million small-acreage farmers around the world each bought a quarter-acre drip system for 50 dollars — a total investment on their part of over 5 billion dollars — it would amount to more than ten times the current annual global sales of drip-irrigation equipment. These 100 million small-plot farmers could put 10 million additional hectares under drip irrigation and increase current global acreage under drip irrigation by a factor of five.

It's laudable that a small but growing number of designers are beginning to develop affordable products because they want to improve the lives of the world's poor. But I think that the best and most sustainable engine for driving the process of designing cheap is this:

Because that's where the money *will be.*

A treadle pump irrigates a seedling nursery.

CHAPTER FIVE

From Subsistence to New Income

"BEFORE YOU STARTED GROWING OFF-SEASON CUCUMBERS AND cauliflower, what did you grow?" I asked Bahadur.

"Rice," he said. "Rice, rice, and then more rice. Rice is how we survive. We have a one-acre rain-fed rice plot down by the river. Before we started growing off-season vegetables, we usually got a good rice crop there between June and September, when it rains a lot, and we still do. If we get a good crop, we store it so we have enough to eat every day for a year."

"What else do you grow?" I asked.

"We grow black gram during the rainy season on our one acre of fields by the house," he said.

I already knew that black gram is a pulse crop that helps provide protein balance for the people who eat it and adds nitrogen to the soil.

"What else?" I asked.

"It's a tradition here to grow vegetables in the rainy season," he said. "We grow sponge gourd, bitter gourd, and beans. The price is so low in the rainy season, it's usually not worth selling vegetables then, but they're very good to eat. Sometimes we can get a good price in the market for sponge gourd and bitter gourd, especially if they have a bad crop in India and not much comes in from there to Nepal.

"In the fall, when there is some rain, we also grow some chilies and onions and other vegetables like that, and we eat most of those too."

"How much money did you make in an average year?" I asked.

This is a question I never ask till we get a chance to talk for a while, because it can be a sensitive one. But usually I manage to get an honest discussion going about income, because I'm there with members of IDE's staff who live in the area and whom the farmers trust.

"Between seven thousand and fifteen thousand rupees [one hundred to two hundred dollars US]," he said, "depending on how much rice we can sell and how much work we can find."

The bottom line is that the harder Bahadur and his family worked, the more things stayed the same. Everything they knew about farming seemed only to keep them running in place. They grew the food they needed to survive, and the traditional ways of growing it were not only ingrained in the culture of their village but were recommended by the government agriculture extension agents they occasionally saw. In fact, most of the people who trained the government extension agents got their degrees from Western universities where they were taught that the best thing small-acreage farmers can do is to grow rice, wheat, and corn for the table so they have enough to eat. Such advice has been standard in the global agricultural community.

"If we can teach small-acreage farmers how to increase their yields of food crops by adopting green revolution strategies," planners in the global agricultural community say, "their lives will improve dramatically. If they adopt green revolution high-yielding varieties of rice, wheat, and corn; increase their fertilizer use; and apply water; they will grow enough to feed their families and have some left over to sell in the market.

"Not only does this increase the local supply of food in grain-deficit areas, but it also allows poor farmers to increase their income by selling their excess production," these experts say.

But this advice ignores a basic piece of information. Even in the West, where the green revolution is in full sway, there are few large-acreage farmers who can earn more than two hundred dollars an acre by growing rice or wheat or corn. Two hundred dollars an acre looks pretty good if you plant two thousand acres of corn, but how much does it do for a farm-family enterprise that has only an acre of land? In fact, limiting the farm output to grains keeps them in perpetual poverty.

The green revolution has transformed world agriculture. Fifty years ago, millions of people in India and China starved to death on a regular basis. The green revolution put a stop to this by dramatically increasing food supply, and China and India are now net grain exporters. But the green revolution failed to put an end to poverty and hunger, much to the dismay of optimistic green revolution planners. Three hundred million people in India and 200 million people in China remain very poor, and most of them still go hungry. Increasing the world's food supply simply eliminates one important factor contributing to hunger. But poverty and hunger will end only when the poor people who live and work on small-farm grassroots enterprises find ways to earn enough money to buy the food they need. Then the market will find ways to bring it to them. When instead, poor, hungry people are placed in a position of long-term reliance on disaster relief, donated food, and government food-distribution systems, their hunger persists.

To achieve results quickly, it was natural for the green revolution to focus first on big farms with good soils and access to irrigation in food-deficit countries like India. But for high-yielding seeds to work their magic, irrigation is essential, and existing irrigation technology is too big to fit on one-acre farms and too expensive to be affordable. So most of the small farms where poverty is centered were left with no irrigation, constraining small-acreage farmers' adoption of high-yielding seeds, and many of the green revolution's positive impacts on food supply and rural jobs and wages were eclipsed by rapid population growth.

In 2005 Norman Borlaug, who received a Nobel Prize for his remarkable contribution to creating the green revolution, was asked what wealthy countries should be doing to reduce hunger in the world. He said they should send food for emergencies, but that the long-range solution is revolutionizing food production, especially among small-acreage subsistence farmers in developing countries. This would not only increase food supply, but would also create jobs and new income from selling excess grain.[22]

Dr. Borlaug's green revolution led us safely across the Malthusian abyss. It's hard to quarrel with success, and when a strategy helps, it is often irresistible to apply more of the same. But more of the same will surely fail to eradicate rural poverty just as it has failed to do so in the past. The subsistence farmers Dr. Borlaug speaks of must now compete effectively in the global marketplace. To do so, they have to play to their strength. Their strength does not lie in trying to compete with two-thousand-acre, mechanized and subsidized prairie wheat farmers in Canada by trying to produce surplus wheat on their one-acre farms.

The unique competitive advantage of small-acreage farmers in the marketplace is that at five to ten cents an hour, they have the lowest labor rates in the world. The most direct way to end the poverty of the 800 million people who live on less than a dollar a day is to increase the income they earn from their one-acre farms. Small-acreage farmers can accomplish this most effectively by growing diversified, labor-intensive, high-value cash crops.

Which brings us back full circle to Krishna Bahadur Thapa and the dead end he faced trying to figure out how to increase the income he and his family could earn from their two-acre farm.

Here is how he found a solution.

From Subsistence to New Cash Income

"If you could stop being poor by earning more from your farm," I said to Bahadur, "how would you go about doing it?"

"I really don't know," he said.

"OK, how do you earn money from your farm now?" I asked.

"I sell rice," he said.

"After the monsoon crop comes in, I usually have twelve hundred to thirteen hundred kilos of rice. I need nine hundred kilos to feed my family, so I sell three hundred kilos to cover the costs of seeds and fertilizer to plant black gram and maize for the next crop and have some cash left over."

"How much does that bring in?" I asked.

"Thirty-five hundred rupees [about $50 US]," he said. "In a really good year, I sell more rice, and maybe a little corn too, and that brings in seven thousand rupees.

"We grow tomatoes and cucumbers and eggplant in the rainy season, but everybody else does too, which brings the price down to the point that selling almost isn't worth it. So we eat most of the vegetables we grow in the rainy season, and sell a few.

"Vegetables sell for three times as much between September and May, because it's too dry for most people to grow them and there aren't any coming into Nepal from India then either. We could make a lot of money here growing vegetables in winter, but we can't do it because we don't have any water for irrigation."

"What other ways do you have to earn money from your farm?" I asked.

"Well, it's not really from the farm. My son and I go into Mugling and try to find a job in one of the guest houses during winter, when there's not much to do on the farm.

"If we can't find decent work in Mugling, we take the bus to Kathmandu or Pokhara and look for work. If we can find jobs there, the pay is a little better, but we have to pay more for food. I have an uncle in Kathmandu who lets us stay. The problem is, sometimes we take the bus to Kathmandu but can't find work, so we come back and try Pokhara, but by the time we find jobs in Pokhara, we've spent a lot on bus fare and eating in Kathmandu. In the end, we usually can clear another thirty-five hundred or six thousand rupees from jobs."

The more I talked to Bahadur, the more I realized that he earned his living from operating a small grassroots enterprise—and a very complicated one at that. This enterprise operates year in and year out on the edge of survival, but somehow Bahadur and his family seem always to make it, even if they may not have enough to eat one year out of three. With negative cash balances and zero reserves, they have to navigate safely through unpredictable floods and droughts and family illnesses, with a hundred critical needs crying out to be paid with the few pennies that are available. Any notion of ending the year with a healthy profit is an impossible dream.

Let's take a closer look at the numbers for Krishna Bahadur Thapa's grassroots family enterprise. Gross annual income is fourteen thousand rupees (two hundred dollars US) from sales of surplus farm products and from wages earned by Bahadur and his son. Expenses for seeds, fertilizer, and pesticides, and for travel, room, and board incurred to earn wage income total thirty-five-hundred rupees, leaving net income for the business of ten thousand five hundred rupees (one hundred fifty dollars US). But family survival expenses for food, clothing, and shelter are also extracted from the family enterprise's income stream. The economic challenges don't spread themselves evenly over the year —both income and expenses usually come in big lumps. There is a big lump in expenses at rice-planting time to pay for land preparation, seeds, and fertilizer, and there is a potential big lump in income at rice-harvest time. So Bahadur and his family face critical decisions at these major income and expense points for their business.

At rice-planting time, they have to decide whether to go for the traditional local variety of rice, which tastes better but has a lower yield, or pick one of the high-yielding varieties that require a much bigger initial investment in seed and fertilizer, will likely produce a 50 percent increase in yield, but which carry with them the risk of incurring a disastrous loss if Bahadur's family is unlucky enough to run into an unexpected flood or pest infestation. If they borrow from a moneylender to pay for the inputs required to grow high-yielding varieties of rice, they may have to pay 80 percent interest at the end of five months, and if the crop fails, how will they pay the money back? If Bahadur is unlucky enough to come down with pneumonia at rice-planting time, how much should they invest in medicines and how much for planting rice? To have any chance at surviving, Bahadur and his family have to apply outstanding skills in managing a business in a perpetual liquidity crisis. To survive, they have learned that the best choice is usually to spend as little money as possible and to desperately avoid risks.

Bahadur and his family just about always come down on the side of playing it safe, although they fully understand the benefits of choices like planting high-value rice. But their decisions are driven by their chronic shortage of capital and by the fact that they simply can't afford to lose. If I buy a penny stock in Denver, Colorado, and it becomes worthless, I complain a lot. But if Bahadur invests more money than he can afford to lose in something like switching to high-yield varieties of rice, and then a rare flood wipes out his crop, he may have sentenced his family to death. If they can't pay back the village moneylender and they lose their farm, they will likely end up begging on the sidewalk in

Kathmandu, and their chances of surviving become far worse than on their small hill farm. For good reasons, when small-farm enterprises like the one Bahadur and his family operate make decisions, they are extremely risk-averse.

Eight hundred million dollar-a-day people now earn their primary income from tiny grassroots farm enterprises, just like Bahadur and his family. Most of them own their own small patches of land, and some earn most of their livelihood as agricultural laborers. Their most direct route to move out of poverty is to increase the net income they earn from small-farm grassroots enterprises where they live and work.

Another 300 million dollar-a-day people live in urban slums or on urban sidewalks. Most of them came to the city to look for work, and they earn their living from a staggering array of grassroots enterprises, ranging from pottery making to garment sweatshops to leather tanning to sweets making. There are as many opportunities to harness the low-cost labor rates of slum dwellers to produce labor-intensive, high-value, marketable products from the grassroots enterprises in urban slums as there are to increase the income of small-acreage farmers by growing and selling labor-intensive, high-value cash crops. But the urban poor have a big advantage. Since they live so close together, the problems of distribution and aggregation, both of inputs and marketable goods, are less than for the scattered and isolated small farms of their rural counterparts.

The kinds of survival grassroots enterprises that offer the best opportunities for dollar-a-day people who live and work in poor rural areas and in slums are not new. They have provided the path to survival for marginalized populations throughout history.

A Short History of Grassroots Enterprises

Grassroots markets are everywhere, and entrepreneurs of all shapes and sizes are their movers and shakers. In Auschwitz, a Jewish physician who was a prisoner traded cigarettes for a small still that had been stolen from warehoused piles of possessions taken from trainloads of people put to death in the gas chambers. The physician put his life on the line by talking some SS guards into letting him use a bag of potatoes. With his small still, he produced a crude form of schnapps that the guards used for their drunken orgies. In return, they gave him the leftover potato mash, which he fried into delicious life-giving patties. He shared some with his close circle of friends, and traded the rest for cigarettes that served as money in camp markets.

Within days after a new refugee camp came to life in Somalia in 1981, women began bartering food and trinkets, displaying them on a patch of dirt bordered by small, whitewashed stones outside their igloo-shaped mud-and-wattle huts. Out-of-work scientists sold watches and household goods in the street markets that sprang up when the Soviet Union's economy collapsed. Thriving cash and barter markets exist in every prison in America, with inmates and sometimes guards participating in a brisk market for drugs.

As a psychiatrist, I was surprised to learn that Willie, a chronic schizophrenic who had lived on the back wards of Dingleton hospital on the Scottish border for twenty years, collected golf balls by stationing himself at the bottom of a hill where he was hidden from the view of foursomes teeing off on the first hole. They experienced a mysteriously high incidence of lost balls, which didn't seem to trouble them on the rest of the course. Willie traded golf balls for broken toasters and electric coffee pots, which he had a remarkable knack for fixing and selling in the village of Melrose.

If Willie, a back-ward schizophrenic, actively participates in markets, and so do concentration camp inmates, prisoners in jails, and refugees in camps, why should it surprise anyone that small-acreage farmers in Ethiopia or Myanmar or people who live in urban slums also make their living in markets? In settings that dictate a daily struggle to survive, people who don't quickly learn how to operate as survival entrepreneurs usually don't make it. If they are small-acreage farmers, they lose their land to the village moneylender and migrate to city slums where things are nearly always worse. If they can't snag a job in the city, even cleaning toilets, they start begging on the sidewalk, but it takes real skill to be a successful beggar, and those who don't have it quickly grow sick and die.

Yet there is an optimistic side to this depressing downward spiral. Slum dwellers and one-acre farmers have the lowest labor rates in the world, and there are vast untapped market opportunities for their grassroots enterprises to grow and prosper.

Mohamed Yunus and the microcredit revolution he has energized have shown that access to credit can be a powerful positive tool. But in any business, access to credit is just one of many critical factors.

To be successful, grassroots enterprises have to be able to implement the same successful business practices as IBM or Toyota or a neighborhood movie house. They have to identify a product or service that customers are willing to pay for that they are uniquely qualified to provide and that they can deliver at a price that customers find attractive. They have to raise the capital they need to succeed and, most importantly, they have to design and implement a highly effective marketing and distribution strategy. At the end of it all, they have to show an attractive profit.

There is no mystery to these principles. Some version of them applies to all successful businesses. But applying them to an enterprise with a gross income of $200 instead of one with an income of $800 million or more requires a radical change in thinking and practice comparable to the difference between driving a nail in a board with a hammer and lifting a one-hundred-ton prefabricated wall into place on a skyscraper with a crane. Increasing income from grassroots enterprises requires a detailed understanding of the strengths and weaknesses of the people who operate them, and of the markets in which they operate. When one considers all the enterprises by which extremely poor people make a living, the most common are tiny farms in poor countries, like the one operated by Bahadur Thapa and his family.

Every member of Bahadur's family is willing and able to work hard just to survive. Their family enterprise is chronically short of cash. Their effective wage rate is between five and ten cents an hour. They have two acres of scattered plots of land. They have no water control for their crops, but they have a monsoon season when more rain falls than they need. The only problem is that during the monsoon season, when they can grow things to sell, everybody else does too, and the prices in the market are so low that they can't make any money selling anything. But they eat well then.

The answer for Bahadur and his family was simple. With the help of IDE and Helvetas, a Swiss development organization, Bahadur's family gained access to a small amount of dependable irrigation water in winter. They had to change their approach to farming by learning methods of intensive horticulture to produce off-season winter cauliflower and cucumbers. They found wholesalers who would buy their crop at an attractive price in the nearby town of Mugling, and traders willing to sell it in the Kathmandu valley. Within two years, Bahadur's family increased their net annual income by thirty-five thousand rupees (five hundred dollars US) and effectively moved out of poverty and into the middle class. How Bahadur and his family accomplished this is probably the most interesting part of the story.

A small-plot farmer in Cambodia

Cambodian woman treadling

CHAPTER SIX

Affordable Small-Plot Irrigation

WHEN KRISHNA BAHADUR THAPA LEARNED THAT HIS UNCLE WHO lived near Pokhara had tripled his income by installing an IDE low-cost drip-irrigation system, Bahadur went to see the system. The drip-irrigation tubes connected to a village water tap that brought water from a spring two kilometers away. The community's water-users' committee had given Bahadur's uncle permission to use some of the system's reserve water capacity.

Bahadur realized immediately that he could do the same thing at home. The drinking water used by twelve families in Ekle Phant had been piped in by Helvetas, a Swiss development organization. In 1999, using a half-inch pipe, Helvetas had provided a constant source of water to each family twenty-four hours a day. This supplied much more than the families needed to meet their household needs but not enough to irrigate crops by flooding their fields. Yet it was more than enough to grow quite a few vegetables if they used a drip system. Bahadur saw that he could marry a drip-irrigation system to the water supply he already possessed.

As we talked, Bahadur and I walked over to take a closer look at his drip system. Water flowed from his half-inch pipe directly into a fifty-liter blue plastic tub that sat on a wooden platform at shoulder height, thus acting as a gravity tank for the system. The water then was directed through a fist-size black plastic filter into a bright green three-eighths-inch-diameter soft plastic tube that split into three fifty-foot lateral lines, each placed on the ground next to a row of plants. Every twelve inches, water dripped out of a tiny baffled hole directly to the cucumber vine beside it, seeping quickly underground to the roots of the plant.

As we talked, Bahadur interrupted his conversation from time to time to point up the hill to the big tank from which his half-inch water pipe came, so of course wild horses couldn't keep me from trudging up to see it. After a fifteen-minute walk along a rocky footpath that wound uphill through dense foliage, we came to a fourteen-thousand-liter enclosed cement water tank about twelve hundred feet from the villagers' homes and sixty-five feet in vertical height above them. Water was diverted from a stream three feet wide and six inches deep into a small dammed reservoir, and from there it flowed through a simple filter and a two-and-a-half-inch plastic pipe into the cement tank. Helvetas had supplied the cement, pipe, and materials for the system, and the villagers had contributed their labor to install it. They all agreed to keep it running under the supervision of a water-users' committee co-chaired by Bahadur.

I walked around the tank and filmed it. I was surprised to find that each family had a separate half-inch, black, high-density polyethylene (HDPE) pipe running from the tank to their individual homes, instead of the cheaper strategy of running one bigger pipe down to the village and then dividing it. Bahadur explained that each family was more comfortable making sure that their own separate line kept flowing.

A back-of-the-envelope calculation estimated that this system cost about twenty-five hundred dollars, which could have been financed easily by a loan instead of a donation from Helvetas, with more than enough income from off-season vegetables to pay back the loan with interest in three years. But at the time when it was built, the system was planned only as a drinking-water system, and without a new source of income, the villagers who used it could afford only to cover its operating costs.

When we went back down the hill for another cup of tea, Bahadur told us that he and his family were the first to install a low-cost drip system in Ekle Phant. In the first year, they planted one-sixteenth acre of drip-irrigated off-season winter cucumber and cauliflower and earned one hundred fifty dollars from it after expenses. That was enough impetus to keep going. They never looked back.

Although the little drip-irrigation system we saw on Bahadur's farm was deceptively simple, it had taken us six years of trial and error to develop it.[23] The biggest challenge was to cut the price of conventional drip systems by four-fifths with sufficient quality to please small-farm customers.

I first got the idea for this after Mr. Upadhiya, the energetic, creative managing director of the Agricultural Development Bank of Nepal (ADBN), had regaled me for two years with stories about the remarkable success of gravity-fed small sprinkler systems promoted by the bank in the hills of Nepal. So in 1990 when we passed through Tanzen, where several of these systems were installed, we stopped at the ADBN branch office unannounced and talked a staff member into taking a half-hour drive and a four-hour walk up steep trails to three villages using these small sprinkler systems.

When we got to the first village, farmers told us these sprinkler systems cost a thousand dollars, served three farmers, and irrigated a total of one acre of fruits and vegetables. I knew right away that this price was too high, making the system unaffordable for most dollar-a-day small-acreage farmers, even when the bank provided a 50 percent subsidy. (By way of comparison, the sprinkler systems designed by IDE India fifteen years later cost two hundred dollars an acre.) So I was curious to learn about the key contributors to the cost of the ADBN's sprinkler systems.

The first sprinkler system we visited collected water overnight from a small stream to fill a three-hundred-fifty-dollar stone-and-cement tank holding ten thousand liters. This was enough to irrigate three farms in the early morning. Water from the tank ran through a filter to a white one-and-a-half-inch six-hundred-fifty-foot-long hard PVC pipe for the three fields and was then delivered to the crops through Rainbird-type oscillating sprinkler heads on shiftable metal stands. Nine sprinkler heads and stands cost one hundred fifty dollars. The fact that the tank had to be sixty feet in vertical height above the field to generate enough pressure to run the sprinklers dictated a long pipe-conveyance system, which was a key contributor to cost.

The immediate challenge was to design a system that would do the same thing at a quarter of the cost. My first idea was to take a piece of cheap black HDPE pipe, punch holes in it with a hammer and a nail, and let the water dribble out through the holes. A small gravity tank sitting two or three feet above the field would provide enough pressure to operate such a drip system. I still have the first plan I drew on my fat Mac computer—a fifty-five-gallon drum sitting in the stream, a little wire-mesh filter, and a black HDPE pipe running fifty feet to the field, where it split into three pipes with holes in them to let the water dribble out to the plants. At this point, of course, I knew little or nothing about drip irrigation, but the idea seemed reasonable enough.

It took us six years and hundreds of field tests to come up with the simple, small, cheap system that Krishna Bahadur Thapa used. It was the last in a series of five generations of low-cost drip systems and hundreds of field tests.[24]

In light of the water-scarcity crisis in many parts of the world and the fact that 70 percent of water diverted for human use goes to irrigation, it is remarkable that drip irrigation represents only 1 percent of irrigated acreage globally, since it is probably the most efficient way of delivering water to plants. Conventional drip irrigation is designed for big farms and costs five times as much per acre as the amount Bahadur paid. The current farms that use drip irrigation are thousand-acre almond tree orchards in California or five-hundred-acre vineyards in France that incorporate data from weather satellites and soil moisture sensors into computer modules that control how much water to apply. These large farms are quite different from the 485 million farms in the world that cultivate less than five acres.

Incredibly, not one of the major drip-irrigation firms in the world has designed drip systems cheap enough and small enough for the majority of the world's farmers, although the potential market dwarfs the demand for conventional systems. In the 1990s no market for drip irrigation existed in Nepal because so few farms were big enough and rich enough to afford it. But there already were fifty private-sector companies fabricating and marketing drip irrigation in India, where there are many big farms that grow high-value crops such as grapes, oranges, and vegetables. I spent a few days with Jain Irrigation, in Maharastra, the biggest drip-irrigation company in India. I asked its biggest-volume dealer the size of the smallest system he had installed in the past year.

"Two acres," he said.

Keep in mind that the average farm size in India at that time was three-and-a-half acres, typically divided into separate plots rarely larger than a half acre, and it becomes clear that few of India's 93 million farms smaller than five acres were getting sales calls from Jain Irrigation dealers. The really poor one-acre farmers weren't even on these dealers' radar.

Since there was no market for drip irrigation in Nepal and the market in India continued to ignore small-acreage farmers, we decided to create a new market for low-cost, small-plot drip irrigation ourselves. By the time Bahadur was ready to buy a low-cost drip system, IDE had convinced several Nepali entrepreneurs with plastics extruders to start fabricating the key components of the system, with assemblers at key village locations putting it together and selling it. We trained local farmers to work part-time as installers. Bahadur bought his system from a local dealer, and received some training on vegetable production from a local IDE agronomist.

When low-cost drip systems became popular among small-plot hill farmers in Nepal, IDE introduced its system to mulberry growers in the silk industry in south India and modified it to fit specific conditions there. Since 2002, sales of low-cost drip systems to both small-plot and larger-acreage farmers have been so brisk that existing companies are entering the low-cost market to compete with the systems introduced by IDE. I believe there is a potential market for at least 5 million low-cost drip-irrigation systems in India alone.

There are hundreds of millions of farmers in the world like Bahadur, farmers who are barely surviving on small, barren patches of land. The great majority of them could dramatically increase their income by growing and selling labor-intensive, high-value cash crops just as Bahadur did. What's stopping them?

The first and most important thing that stands in the way of these farmers is that most of them, not having a way to apply water to their crops, depend on rainfall. This usually means they can grow food for the table during the rainy season. They can grow cash crops like vegetables during the rainy season, but everybody else grows them then too, and the market price is so low they're usually not worth selling. The way to make money is to grow cash crops during the off-season, when prices are much higher; but it can't be done without irrigation, and the irrigation tools that are available in the world are too big and too expensive to fit their small plots. To increase their income as Bahadur did, small-acreage farmers need access to affordable small-plot irrigation.

So why is it that affordable small-plot irrigation isn't available?

An experience I had in Mozambique goes a long way toward answering this question. I was visiting the vegetable markets in the capital town of Maputo, and they were absolutely huge. I make a habit of measuring the shelf space apportioned to different fruits and vegetables in markets, and there were endless rows of tomatoes, potatoes, lettuce, kale, chili peppers, onions—just about anything one could want. But when I asked the vendors where each vegetable came from, I got a depressingly uniform answer: South Africa. These products were trucked in, a trip taking about five hours on decent highways from South Africa, off-loaded to trucks from Mozambique at the border, and sold to supply the burgeoning demand for vegetables in the capital city.

I was puzzled because it seemed to me that there was plenty of good land, and even irrigation, within two hours of bumpy roads from Maputo. So I talked to the experts in agriculture and irrigation in Maputo. One expatriate with a PhD in irrigation, author of numerous publications, told me in no uncertain terms that there just was no irrigation available within striking distance of Maputo. I left his office, hailed a taxi, and asked the driver if there was any irrigation going on around Maputo.

"Certainly, sir—would you like me to take you there?" he replied.

"How far is it?" I asked.

"About fifteen minutes," he said. "It's right next to the beer factory."

In twelve minutes, we pulled up to a five-hundred-acre green area exploding with vegetables, and I got out and filmed it. There must have been eight hundred individual plots, and most were a beehive of activity. A small river ran close to this vegetable-producing area, and one of the previous socialist governments had set up a station that pumped water to small cement aboveground open cisterns that were two-and-a-half feet deep and six feet on each side. Most of these small-plot farms had such a cistern, and the pumping system kept them full.

The farmers took two sprinkling cans, filled them by dunking them in the tanks, and lugged the cans, one in each hand, to their vegetable plots to sprinkle their vegetables. Then they came back for more. Some of them used wooden shoulder bars, which made the carrying easier. Some families who didn't have a cistern hauled directly from the river, even though it meant they had a longer carry. They were growing onions, tomatoes, and every other kind of vegetable, but apparently they sold their produce in smaller neighborhood markets instead of the big markets I had visited. Impressed, I tried to calculate the cost to build a thousand systems like this and what the relative cost would be to fill them by a gravity feed.

Later that day, I went back to the irrigation expert's office. "I thought you said there was no irrigation within striking distance of Maputo," I said, with a trace of indignation in my voice.

"That's right," he said.

"Well, I just visited five hundred irrigated acres fifteen minutes from here," I declared.

"Where was that?" he asked.

"Right next to the brewery," I said.

"Oh yes, I know about those vegetable fields," he said. "But of course, that's not irrigation."

"Why not?" I asked.

"Because they use buckets," he said, and he made it clear that our conversation was over.

"I thought irrigation was bringing water to plants!" I said. And then the conversation really was over.

What's even worse than the fact that this conversation actually took place is the fact that his attitude is endemic among officially declared irrigation experts and the leaders of development institutions.

In 1995 Gez Cornish—from the respected UK water-consulting firm HR Wallingford—and his team carried out a three-year study of informal bucket irrigation supplying vegetables to the city of Kumasi (population seven hundred thousand) in Ghana. The study concluded that at least twelve thousand seven hundred households grew vegetables for Kumasi, and that these vegetables provided the biggest part of their yearly income. The study concluded that at least 11,900 hectares (29,750 acres) were irrigated by informal methods around Kumasi.[25]

However, when the Food and Agriculture Organization (FAO, a global Rome-based UN agriculture institution) delivered its formal report on irrigation in Ghana, a report then accepted as gospel by the government of Ghana, it listed a total of only *sixty-four hundred* irrigated hectares in all of Ghana! This is about half of the acreage under bucket irrigation in a single city in Ghana. Does this sound familiar? For experts in Ghana, no less than for the irrigation expert I talked to in Mozambique, bucket irrigation simply doesn't exist. How unfortunate that this represents mainstream thinking in irrigation.

Of course, government officials display the same attitude toward rickshaws in Bangladesh—they see them as primitive, backward, and embarrassing modes of transport at a time when Bangladesh is trying to present itself to the outside world as a modern country, even though these humble rickshaws move more people and cargo in one day than does the London underground.[26]

Why does the world continue to close its eyes to the reality of both one-acre farms and small-plot irrigation? It's because subsistence farms and the bucket irrigation that they often use are seen as backward and primitive, ripe for replacement by modern agriculture and modern irrigation.

Nobody seems to know how many people irrigate by bucket in Africa, or in China, or in Vietnam, although I have seen thousands of them with my own eyes. On this topic, no official statistics are available. So here's an unofficial estimate. I asked ten people who have done a lot of traveling in rural areas how many bucket farmers they think there are in Africa. The lowest estimate I got was 8 million.

The small-plot farmers all over the world have consistently told me that the single most important thing they need in order to move out of poverty is water for their crops. I made the design and mass marketing of affordable small-plot irrigation tools the first focus of IDE when I started it in 1981.

Access to Water

When I tell people that the most important thing small-acreage farmers need in order to move out of poverty is access to affordable small-plot irrigation, listeners usually say to me that I am fighting a losing battle. Most poor farmers simply have no access to water.

"That's not true," I say. "Everybody in the world has access to water. People with no access to water die within five days. Everyone in the world who breathes in and out has access to water. It may be polluted water, or loaded with bacteria. But without a source of water to drink, people die.

"To get irrigation started, all it takes is an extra two buckets of water a day from the same source where you get your drinking water. That is enough to grow a small vegetable garden with a three-dollar drip kit and earn nine dollars by selling surplus vegetables.

"Of course, in some places, the water is so scarce that all of it has to be used for drinking. But if there are two buckets a day to spare per family for income-generating plants, there is an opportunity to start irrigating."

There are many other big untapped opportunities for small-acreage farmers to gain access to a source of water for irrigation.

There are, in fact, practical ways to address the problem of small-farm access to water. From the largest to the smallest, the irrigation tools can be classified as water-lifting, water-storage, and water-distribution technologies.

Water Lifting

Some irrigation systems store monsoon rainwater behind big dams and release it to flow by gravity through canals to farmers' fields, bypassing the need to lift it. Groundwater has been an increasingly important source of water for irrigation, and in big irrigation systems, big diesel or electric engines drive pumps that bring water from below the ground to the surface, where it is delivered to plants in a variety of ways.

But in the 485 million farms in the world that are smaller than five acres, most of the groundwater that is brought to the surface is raised by the farmer's manual labor. Some use a bucket on a rope. Others use a bucket suspended from a horizontal pole with a weight on the other end as a counterbalance to equalize the work of raising and lowering the bucket. Still others use a bullock pulling a twenty-five-gallon bladder attached to a rope passing over a windlass to the water in an open well.

Buckets, counterbalanced buckets, sprinkling cans, and swing baskets are cheap but require a lot of muscle power. Of course, this is a renewable form of energy.

Until the design and mass marketing of treadle pumps, there were few tools for small-acreage farmers to use to lift water, between the extremes of, at one end, a bucket, which is very cheap and too small, and at the other end, a five-horsepower diesel pump, which is very expensive and too big. It takes a healthy man a day to lift enough water with a rope and bucket to irrigate an eighth of an acre of vegetables, and another two days to carry it to his crops in sprinkling cans. If he has enough money to pay five hundred dollars for a five-hp diesel pump and can afford two hundred dollars a year in diesel fuel and repairs to keep it running, he can keep five acres of vegetables watered without much trouble. But this is hard to do on a total income of three hundred dollars a year.

TREADLE PUMPS

In the 1980s Gunnar Barnes, a Norwegian engineer working for Rangpur Dinajpur Rural Service (RDRS), a rural development organization in northern Bangladesh sponsored by Lutheran World Service, designed the treadle pump, a human-powered water-lifting device that a small-plot farmer could buy with a sack of rice. The operator treads on two bamboo treadles, each of which activates a two-and-a-half-inch cylinder that sucks up water from a tube well with a depth of six to twenty-five feet. Since groundwater over most of Bangladesh lies shallow, treadle pumps can be used to lift water in the dry winter season. The pump itself retails for eight dollars, and the total cost of a pump installed on a tube well by a village well-driller is twenty-five dollars. With this investment and two to six hours of labor a day, a family could irrigate a half-acre of vegetables during the dry season, earning an average of at least one hundred dollars a year after expenses. Best of all, the one-fifth or so of small-acreage farmers who were more market-savvy regularly earned new net income of more than five hundred dollars a year.

IDE worked with Gunnar Barnes and RDRS to take over the national marketing and promotion of treadle pumps through the private sector, and after twelve years, this produced remarkably positive impacts.

Donor investment in TP initiative	$12 million
Smallholder investment in TP	$37.5 million
Annual net smallholder return on investment	$150 million

Table 4: Impact of Treadle Pumps (TP) in Bangladesh

These impacts did not stop in Bangladesh. IDE introduced treadle pumps at an unsubsidized price through private-sector enterprises in India, Nepal, Cambodia, Myanmar, and Zambia, and many other organizations took up the challenge as well. KickStart, headquartered in Kenya, brought treadle pumps from Bangladesh to Kenya, redesigned them for local use, and sold some seventy thousand in Kenya and Tanzania. Enterprise Works Worldwide, another development organization, made and marketed treadle pumps in West African countries such as Niger.

These 2.25 million treadle pumps are generating more than $200 million new net annual income for dollar-a-day small-acreage farmers. Then there is a multiplier impact on village economies in the range of $600 million per year. In parts of Bangladesh and India, the influx of new income, coupled with a drop in the price of diesel pumps imported from China to below $200, has created a rapid uptake of low-cost diesel pumps and the creation of efficient water markets as diesel-pump owners sell surplus irrigation water in the marketplace. Happily, these water markets are now providing effective competition with treadle pumps to bring affordable irrigation water to small-acreage farmers in Bangladesh and India.

ROPE-AND-WASHER PUMPS

Adding a component to treadle pumps that pushes water to the suction unit creates a pressure treadle pump that can pump up to sixty feet, but it costs twice as much as the suction pump and pumps less water because it takes more work to pump from depth. But the rope-and-washer pump, developed in Nicaragua, can lift water as much as a hundred feet. This is a pump based on pulling a rope upward through a pipe in the well, with washers attached to the rope. As an operator on the surface turns a crank, the rope is drawn up through the pipe, carrying water to the top. Some sixty thousand of these rope-and-washer pumps have been sold in Nicaragua, primarily for household water. Rope-and-washer pumps are now being tested in conjunction with low-cost drip systems to make the comparatively small amount of water that can be lifted from depth with human power irrigate enough plants to be economically attractive.

MICRODIESEL PUMPS

When it comes to nonelectric motorized pumps, diesel pumps have advantages over gasoline engine–powered pumps because they last

Organization	Country	Treadle Pump Sales to Date	Current Annual Sales	Total Sales
IDE	Bangladesh	1,567,987	40,000	2,071,763
	India	353,542	15,000	
	Nepal	100,000	10,000	
	Cambodia	38,578	1,200	
	Myanmar	7,000	7,000	
	Zambia	4,656	800	
KickStart	Kenya & Tanzania	59,000	NA	59,250
	Mali	250	NA	
EnterpriseWorks	Senegal	600	NA	17,181
	Tanzania	131	NA	
	Niger	1,200	NA	
	Burkina Faso	15,250	NA	
Government of Malawi	Malawi	75,000	NA	75,000
Total				2,223,194

Table 5: Global Treadle Pump Sales

longer and use less fuel. The ideal size of a diesel pump that would fit a one-acre farm is about three-quarters of a horsepower, but until now, the smallest diesel pump was a two-horsepower, commercially available from China. Right after World War II, a three-quarter-horsepower air-cooled microdiesel operating through a friction wheel on the front tire of bicycles was used to boost bicycle power in Europe. IDE and Practica, a Dutch development organization, are now working on prototypes of the three-quarter-horsepower bicycle-powering microdiesels modified to drive a water pump. If this proves effective, there is a probable global market demand for several million microdiesels from one-acre farmers who have earned enough income to invest in mechanized water-lifting tools.

Water Storage

In most places in the world, even the dry ones, most of the year's rain falls during the two to four months of the monsoon season. In the hot, dry climate of the state of Maharastra in India, for example, small-acreage farmers' fields become quagmires in late summer. After that, it becomes hotter and drier until before the monsoon, when temperatures rise to one hundred twelve degrees Fahrenheit in the shade. This is when market prices for fruits and vegetables reach their highest levels, but there is no hope of producing a crop without irrigation.

IDE is now designing a four-hundred-dollar plastic-lined pond with plastic cover, thirty-five feet in length and width and seven feet deep. This low-cost small-farm water-storage system will hold two hundred thousand liters of monsoon rainwater, enough to drip-irrigate a quarter acre of high-value vegetables during the driest time of the year for one hundred days and generate five hundred dollars in new net income.

At the other end of the scale is Lake Nasser, the lake behind Aswan Dam, three hundred thirty miles long and twenty-one miles wide, with a surface area of more than 4 million acres. About 7 percent of the water diverted for human use is lost from evaporation from reservoirs behind big dams. In the world of dams, a big dam is anything over fifteen meters high (about fifty feet). Dams less than fifteen

Low-cost water storage: This ten-meter-by-one-meter-diameter double-walled plastic cylinder, supported by an earthen trench, holds twenty-five hundred gallons of water.

meters high are classified as small dams. Dollar-a-day farmers rarely see a dam higher than two meters, if they see one at all.

Of course, small-acreage farmers like Bahadur don't need a dam. He is lucky enough to have a stream running all year that brings him a half-inch pipe full of water twenty-four/seven. Most one-acre farmers in Bangladesh have groundwater ten or fifteen feet down during the dry season, and all they have to do is to suck it out with a device such as a treadle pump.

But farmers who lack access to either a stream or shallow groundwater may need to trap monsoon rainwater and store it for six months until the driest time of year when crop prices are at their peak. For them, the critical question is "How much water do I need to store to be able to earn five hundred dollars?"

The answer is pretty straightforward. You can just about always clear five hundred dollars from a quarter acre (one thousand square meters) of fruits and vegetables during the hottest and driest time of year, and in most places, small-plot farmers would need to store two hundred thousand liters or so in an enclosed tank to drip-irrigate a quarter acre of vegetables for a hundred days during the dry season.

The irony is that even before biblical times, people were trapping, gathering, and storing rainwater for later use. In the Yellow River Basin of China, hand-dug underground cisterns lined with clay have been used for more than a thousand years to store monsoon rainfall collected by contoured runoff channels. Millions of these "dry wells" are still in use, taking advantage in modern times of runoff from roadbeds, and using some of the stored water for irrigation. But aside from Chinese dry wells, which cost about one hundred fifty dollars for a ten-thousand-liter storage system, there just aren't any available practical models that can store two hundred thousand liters of irrigation water in an enclosed tank and be cheap enough for small-acreage farmers to afford.

I believe a four-hundred-dollar plastic-lined enclosed storage system will be purchased by millions of small-plot farmers around the world.

Here are some other options for one-acre farmers who don't have access to dry-season streams, springs, lakes, or near-the-surface groundwater.

STORE WATER UNDERGROUND

The best storage reservoir may be in underground sand layers called "aquifers." In the 1980s, a Hindu religious movement, Swadhyaya Parivar, led thousands of farmers in Gujarat to build waterways that direct monsoon runoff into large open wells. This collective action restored groundwater aquifers and made the stored water available for pumping to the surface during the dry season when crop prices are at their peak. There is a huge untapped potential for directing monsoon rainwater into underground aquifers, where it can be stored without any loss to evaporation and pumped out again during the time of year when prices for fruits and vegetables are at their peak.

STORE WATER ABOVEGROUND

1. **Build a pond.** Any self-respecting small-acreage farmer knows how to build a hundred-square-meter pond that is two meters

deep. The key to making it effective and affordable is to line it with plastic that prevents leaking and lasts at least two or three years. If the water is stored for several months, farmers need to find ways to eliminate or decrease evaporation. Shade provided by trees or by bamboo poles covered with banana or other broad leaves helps, and IDE is now designing a low-cost plastic cover to eliminate surface evaporation.

2. **Create a low-cost water tank.** The giant condom solution: To prevent evaporation, the ideal form of storage is an enclosed tank. But the cheapest ferro-cement tank costs a rupee a liter (slightly more than two cents US) in India. To lower this cost, IDE in India has designed and field-tested a ten-meter-long, one-meter-diameter, double-walled plastic tube in an earthen trench (see page 108). The tube costs forty dollars and stores ten thousand liters of water. This is enough to provide drinking water for a family of five for a year and have some left over for a small drip-irrigated kitchen garden. Initial market tests for the enclosed plastic tube are taking place in India in 2007.

The wading pool solution: A creative student design team at Stanford came up with an even simpler solution for a low-cost aboveground, enclosed water-storage system. They took the design of a simple plastic wading pool as a starting point. This is a plastic container shaped a bit like an upside-down bowler hat. As the storage container is filled, the water pressure pushes against the side walls and gives shape to it. Since the mechanical forces acting on the side walls are a function of the depth, there should be no limitation in size. The side-wall forces for a two-foot-deep wading pool remain the same if it increases in size from three feet by four feet to nine feet by twelve feet.

A farmer running a gravity pipe from a stream can roll up the plastic wading pool like a bedroll and carry it to the part of the field he or she wants to irrigate. If he has a thousand-liter wading pool, all he has to do is fill it with a pipe from the stream and run another pipe from the pool to the low-cost drip-irrigation system.

Now, I say all this without knowing if it will actually work. The student team and IDE Myanmar are still testing it in the field.

Water Distribution

Since 70 percent of water diverted for human use in the world goes to irrigation, the astonishing fact is that some 90 percent of irrigation water is applied to fields and crops using inefficient surface methods that have been used unchanged for the past eight hundred years. In most canal systems, there are huge water losses through seepage between the source and the field. An unintended consequence is that the leakage restores shallow aquifers, allowing many small farms to install shallow wells and pumps delivering irrigation water on demand. But when it comes to delivering this water to their crops, farmers usually apply the inefficient surface methods everyone else uses.

After a small-acreage farmer has painstakingly collected and stored water in a two-hundred-cubic-meter pond, he needs an efficient water-distribution system to get the water to his crops without using it all up in the first day's irrigation. He needs low-cost drip-irrigation systems that ensure that 80 or 90 percent of the precious stored water goes right to the roots of the plants, or something equally efficient. For other crops, low-cost, low-pressure sprinkler systems, while not quite as efficient as drip systems, are much more efficient than conventional surface irrigation. But conventional drip and sprinkler systems simply are not available at a price a dollar-a-day farmer can afford and at a size that fits that farmer's typical quarter-acre plots.

LOW-COST DRIP IRRIGATION

I've already described affordable small-plot drip-irrigation systems and their potential for reaching at least 10 million one-acre farmers over the next ten or fifteen years (see Figure 1).

LOW-COST SPRINKLER SYSTEMS

Small-acreage farmers use low-cost, low-pressure sprinklers instead of low-cost drip systems for plants that aren't in rows or closely spaced, for hilly fields, and when water is loaded with minerals that clog drip-irrigation systems. When Jack Keller started working on the design of small-plot, low-cost sprinkler systems, his first step was finding sprinkler heads capable of distributing water uniformly at five meters of pressure generated by water flowing from a tank five meters above the ground. At that time, the standard pressure head needed for conventional sprinkler systems was twenty meters. These IDE low-cost sprinkler systems are just emerging from field-testing in India, and will cost about eighty dollars for a half-acre system.

A RANGE OF NEW AFFORDABLE SMALL-PLOT IRRIGATION TOOLS

I have described a few of the affordable small-plot irrigation tools that are being developed. They represent only the tip of the iceberg. Other tools—such as affordable well-drilling and -construction technology;

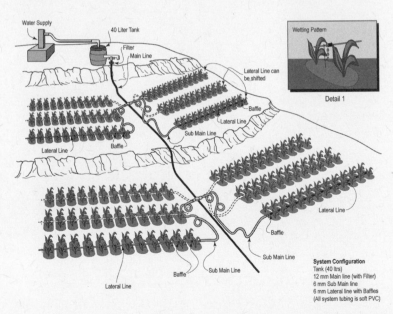

Figure 1. Schematic of a 1990s-vintage IDE low-cost microtube drip-irrigation system

low-cost, efficient small-plot surface irrigation; and the development of total rainwater harvesting, storage, and application systems for one-acre farms—are waiting to be developed.

What Is Next?

Without access to a source of water from the year-round stream and a low-cost drip system to bring it to his cucumbers, Bahadur could never have escaped from poverty. Access to affordable small-plot irrigation was a necessary, but not a sufficient, condition. To earn enough to lift themselves out of poverty, Bahadur and his family needed to learn about a new field of intensive cash-crop agriculture and how to sell their crops in the marketplace at a profit.

In Nepal, a gravity tank irrigates off-season cucumbers.
The woman is filling the tank with a pipe delivering water
from a stream above the field.

CHAPTER SEVEN

A New Agriculture for One-Acre Farms

"BIG FAT GREEN CUCUMBERS!" SAID KRISHNA BAHADUR THAPA emphatically as he embraced a green armful lovingly.

I had asked him what the key was to his first big bump in income. Then, of course, we had no choice but to follow him respectfully into his field, watch as he snipped far more cucumbers than we would ever be able to eat, and admire each one of them. Then we had to chow down on slice after slice—but not before he garnished each one with a delicate sprinkling of salt.

These lightly salted cucumber slices tasted juicy and slightly bitter to me, but nothing special. They were just fresh cucumbers. But to Nepalis in the middle of the hot, dry winter, there was something magical about them. Their juiciness seemed to belie the parched landscape, and most Nepalis attributed healing and illness-preventing powers to them. In the market at Mugling, cucumbers sold for thirty to forty rupees a kilo (about forty-five cents US) between January and May, three times the normal price of ten rupees per kilo, because Indian farmers couldn't grow cucumbers in winter and few Nepali farmers had access to irrigation water in the dry season. We saw eight- and ten-year-olds dressed in tatters hawking cucumber slices at bus stops, and along the road to Kathmandu at a spring with cool water where everybody stopped for a drink, a little shop with bamboo walls and a banana-leaf roof sold them at three times the normal price.

So when it came to deciding what to plant in January, right after he had borrowed half of the thirty-six dollars he needed to buy and install his first sixteenth-acre drip system, for Bahadur it was a no-brainer.

Cucumbers!

The first step was to borrow an ax from a neighbor, hike up into the forest above Bahadur's house, and carry down shoulder-load after shoulder-load of gnarled trees and branches, each about ten feet high. Then he dug them deep into the ground in rows four feet apart, with three feet between each of the dead trees. This skeletal forest was a permanent installation. It provided the structural support for the cucumber vines planted in January, but he did not take down the branches at the end of cucumber season in May. This dead forest provided the climbing space for the sponge gourds, bitter gourds, and beans Bahadur and his family would grow during the monsoon season from June to September, earning another decent profit.

When I talked to Bahadur and his family two years after they harvested their first crop of drip-irrigated cucumbers, they had expanded their off-season drip-irrigated vegetable enterprise to one thousand square meters (a quarter acre) and were clearing a steady five hundred to six hundred dollars a year from their one-acre farm, instead of the unpredictable fifty to one hundred fifty dollars of prior years. They still grew rice on their one-acre rain-fed field by the river in the June–September monsoon season, and they followed it with black gram and some maize. They rotated black gram, maize, and a few other crops on some of their upland fields as well. They felt comfortable now devoting more of their fields to growing high-value cash crops in place of focusing only on rice, black gram, and maize, the crops that fed the family but earned little or no income.

The crop rotation on their newly drip-irrigated quarter acre looked something like this:

From January through May, they grew cucumbers, from which they earned a net profit of seventeen thousand rupees (about two hundred

Deu Bahadur Thapa stands with his trellised monsoon-season crop, just as his father did a few years before.

dollars). When the monsoon season came, they planted bitter gourds, sponge gourds, and beans in the same field, which used the same dead branches to climb. I was surprised to hear that they even used the drip-irrigation system occasionally during the monsoon season during gaps in the rain. They earned another seventeen thousand rupees from selling beans, bitter gourds, and sponge gourds.

In the season from September through December, when it rained intermittently, they earned another four thousand rupees (sixty dollars or so) by growing off-season cauliflower and selling it to traders who came to the farm. They made another fifty dollars from chilies, onions, and assorted vegetables, but ate at least half of these vegetables themselves.

By switching the emphasis of their small-farm grassroots enterprise from subsistence crops to high-value cash crops, they found themselves propelled almost overnight from bare survival to becoming part of a fast-growing middle class in Nepal. And they were determined to keep learning.

Cucumbers growing
on trellised vines in
Nepal

Learning to grow off-season cucumbers and cauliflower took three
months of training by an IDE agronomist who came to the village
every two weeks on his bicycle. He demonstrated how to raise cucumber
seedlings in a low-cost, two-foot-high, plastic-tunnel greenhouse after
sterilizing the soil bed, and explained the mixtures of nutrients and
micronutrients to apply at different stages of the plant growth cycle.

Small Farms Are Very Big

Surprisingly, small farms like Bahadur's play a much bigger role in
global agriculture than most people realize. For twenty of the twenty-
five years I worked with small-acreage farmers, I underestimated the
importance of small farms in world agriculture. I knew how important
they were for poverty, but I assumed they represented only 10 or 15 percent of farmland. I was astonished to learn how important they are.

I was not alone. The leaders in universities where courses in agriculture are taught, and organizations that fund, plan, and implement
agriculture initiatives have underestimated the huge role that farms
smaller than two acres play in poverty and the role that farms smaller
than five acres play in the agricultural productivity of the planet.

What Oksana Nagayets, a research analyst at the International Food Policy Research Institute (IFPRI), found when she prepared a background paper on small farms in 2005[27] is remarkable.

Of the 525 million farms in the world, *445 million, some 85 percent, are smaller than five acres.* Farms under five acres (two hectares) represent 95 percent of the farms and 69 percent of the total cultivated area in Bangladesh, and they represent 87 percent of farms and 60 percent of total cultivated area in Ethiopia. In China, 98 percent of all farms are smaller than five acres (see Table 6).[28]

The average farm size in both Asia and Africa is now 1.6 hectares (3.75 acres) (see Table 7).[29] The farms cultivated by dollar-a-day families are much smaller than the 4-acre average. Farm size in the United States and Europe, where much of the leadership of global agricultural research institutions originates, is dramatically higher and continues to rise, while farm size in developing countries continues to fall (Table 8).[30]

In spite of the predictions of economists, average farm size in developing countries steadily decreased (Table 8),[31] probably because of rapid population growth. Average farm size in the United States and in just about every country in Europe, however, is steadily increasing, just as economists predict.

It is clear that small farms comprise a surprisingly high portion of total cultivated acreage in developing countries (see Table 9).[32]

Farms less than five acres contributed 40 percent of food-grain production and dominated the dairy sector in India in 1990-91; they made up 49 percent of total agricultural production in Kenya in 1985. As of 2005, small-plot farmers contributed 85 percent of total agricultural production in Malawi and 97 percent of milk production in Ethiopia. In Russia in 2001, farms less than five acres produced 51 percent of the milk, 57 percent of the meat, 80 percent of the vegetables, 93 percent of the potatoes, and 28 percent of the eggs.[33]

The Size of Dollar-a-Day Farms

If there are 445 million small farms and a family of five lives on each of them, then 2.2 billion of the 6.2 billion people in the world live and work on small farms. But the farms on which 800 million people earn a living

Country	Census year	Number of farms under 2 hectares	Share of farms under 2 hectares, percent
Asia			
China	1997	189,394,000	98
India	1995–96	92,822,000	80
Indonesia	1993	17,268,123	88
Bangladesh	1996	16,991,032	96
Vietnam	2001	9,690,506	95
Africa			
Ethiopia	2001–02	9,374,455	87
Nigeria	2000	6,252,235	74
DR Congo	1990	4,351,000	97
Tanzania	1994–95	2,904,241	75
Egypt	1990	2,616,991	90
Americas			
Mexico	1991	2,174,931	49
Peru	1994	1,004,668	58
Brazil	1996	983,330	21
Ecuador	1999–2000	366,058	43
Venezuela	1996–97	133,421	23
Europe			
Russia*	2002	16,000,000	98
Ukraine	2003	6,214,800	99
Romania	1998	2,279,297	58
Bulgaria	1998	1,691,696	95
Poland	2002	1,494,100	51

Sources: Calculated by Nagayets based on FAO (2001, 2004) and data from national statistical agencies. Reproduced with permission of IFPRI (see Notes, page 214).

*Data are based on farm size of less than 1 hectare.

Table 6: Top Five Countries with the Largest Number of Small Farms, by Region

World region	Average farm size, hectares
Africa	1.6
Asia	1.6
Latin America and Caribbean	67.0
Europe*	27.0
North America	121.0

Source: von Braun 2005. Reproduced with permission of IFPRI (see Notes, page 214). *Data include Western Europe only.

Table 7: Approximate Farm Size by World Region

of a dollar a day or less are much smaller than five acres—typically one acre divided into four or five scattered plots. The several thousand dollar-a-day farms I have visited range from a hundredth of an acre in peri-urban areas of densely populated countries to ten acres in dry regions, but their usual size is one acre.

Small Farms and Modern Agriculture

If 85 percent of all the farms in the world are smaller than five acres and if they produce more than half the crops, meat, and dairy products in most developing countries, then surely most of the cutting-edge research in agriculture in the world is centered on improving productivity and income of small farms, right?

Wrong!

Why should leaders in agriculture consistently overlook the importance of small farms?

The answer isn't mysterious.

The centers of expertise in agriculture, where future leaders in developing countries come for their training, are in the United States, a country where the average farm size in 2002 was four hundred forty-six acres, and in Europe, where the average farm size in 2005 was sixty-eight acres. It is perfectly natural for professors in Western universities, who do most of their PhD research on Western farms, to see everything in the context that is familiar to them and of where they do their

Country	Census year	Average farm size, hectares	Total area of holdings, hectares	Number of farms under 2 hectares
Selected developed countries				
United States	1969	157.6	430,321,000	108,370
	2002	178.4	379,712,151	NA
United Kingdom	1970	55.1	17,992,312	NA
	1993	70.2	17,144,777	NA
Austria	1969	20.7	7,490,463	75,840
	1990	26.7	7,217,498	38,694
Germany	1971	14.2	15,236,139	195,198
	1995	30.3	17,156,900	90,600
Selected developing countries				
DR Congo	1970	1.5	3,821,916	2,026,740
	1990	0.5	2,387,700	4,351,000
Ethiopia	1977	1.4	6,862,200	3,675,500
	2001–02	1.0	11,047,249	9,374,455
China	1980	0.6	NA	NA
	1999	0.4	NA	NA
India	1971	2.3	162,124,000	49,114,000
	1991	1.6	165,507,000	84,480,000
	1995–96	1.4	163,357,000	92,822,000
Indonesia	1973	1.1	16,394,000	12,712,791
	1993	0.9	17,145,036	17,268,123
Nepal	1992	1.0	2,598,971	2,407,169
	2002	0.8	2,654,037	3,083,241
Pakistan	1971–73	5.3	19,913,000	1,059,038
	2000	3.1	20,437,554	3,814,798

Source: Calculated by Nagayets based on FAO (2001, 2004). Data for China are from Fan and Chan-Kang (2003). Reproduced with permission of IFPRI (see Notes, page 214).

Note: NA indicates that data were not available.

Table 8: Trends in Average Farm Size and Number of Small Farms

research. It is also natural for them to be influenced by the professors around them who regard small farms and the simple tools used on them as embarrassing Stone Age aberrations that will soon be replaced by bigger farms as market forces progress.

It is unlikely that their students will learn anything at all about how to raise three goats in a hill village in Nepal or how to grow a quarter acre of off-season vegetables in a tribal village in India and make money doing it. While large-farm-centered agriculture applies perfectly well

	Number of small farms as a share of total farms (percent)	Share of total area cultivated by smallholders (percent)
Egypt 1990[a]	75	49
Ethiopia 1999/2000	87	60
DR Congo 1990	97	86
Uganda 1991	73	27
Bangladesh 1996	95	69
India 1995/1996	80	36
Indonesia 1993	88	55
Nepal 2002	92	69
Pakistan 2000	58	15
Brazil 1996	20	0.3
Ecuador 1990/2000	43	2
Panama 2001[b]	53	0.6
Georgia 1998	96	33
Poland 2002	51	7
Romania 1998	58	14
Russia 2002[b]	98	3
Ukraine 2003	99	8

Source: FAO 2001, 2004; Tanic 2001, Goskomstat 2002, World Bank/OECD 2004. Reproduced with permission of IFPRI (see Notes, page 214).

a. Less than 2.1 hectares.

b. Less than 1 hectare.

Table 9: Small Farms as a Share of Total Number of Farms and Total Cultivable Area

to the Western farm context, such processes are tragically wrong when they are applied willy-nilly to developing countries. There, farms are tiny and steadily getting tinier, and the smaller and more remote they are, the more likely they are to be occupied by people who survive on less than a dollar a day. If I were the dictator of world agriculture for a day, I would insist that every candidate for a master's or a PhD degree in agriculture be required to implement a six-month research study addressing agricultural problems on one-acre farms. We would see a revolution in thinking and practice for poverty-related agriculture.

In the mid 1980s, I gave a talk at Cornell on IDE's work, and two agricultural engineering professors berated me for promoting treadle pumps, which they said forced people to perform coolie labor when modern machines were available to liberate them from their drudgery. When IDE was helping refugees build and sell five hundred donkey carts in Somalia, a government official there who had a PhD from Boston criticized me publicly for trying to implement a donkey cart project.

"Dr. Polak," he asked, "do you take a donkey cart to your office in Denver every morning? How dare you recommend donkey carts to us? We have been using donkey carts since before you were born, and now we are trying to modernize our country."

Of course, two years later when the donkey cart project was the most successful income-generating program in Somalia, he saw things differently.

Small Farms and Agricultural Innovation

The green revolution held great promise for small farms. But to grow the new high-yielding varieties of rice, wheat, and maize, small-acreage farmers had to gain access to irrigation, fertilizer, and the cultivation methods required for these new miracle crops to flourish. Seeds are easy to divide into small packages. But growing one kilo of grain requires a thousand kilos of water. Large canal systems supply sufficient water to grow rice, wheat, and corn, but it is much more difficult to split irrigation equipment into small pieces than it is to divide a kilo of rice seeds into six-ounce packages. Constrained access to affordable small-plot irrigation has been a major barrier to adoption of green revolution seeds and strategies by farmers with scant farmland, so most of them, like Bahadur, grow their grain crops in the monsoon season, when there is a higher risk of catastrophic floods.

But there is another important constraint. Since dollar-a-day farmers are chronically cash-poor, they have trouble coming up with fifty dollars or so to cover the costs of green revolution seeds, fertilizer, and pesticides. Even if they find the money, small-plot farmers are reluctant to invest more in inputs than they can afford to lose in an every-ten-years flood. This risk goes away if they can grow rice in the dry season, but it takes irrigation to do so.

The upshot of all this is that although the green revolution has increased rice yields to five to six tons per hectare in places like Japan and Taiwan, most dollar-a-day small-plot farmers plant open-pollinated traditional varieties of rice which require less fertilizer, present less risk, and will produce a reasonable rain-fed crop with yields in the one-to-three-tons-per-hectare range. The new biogenetic seeds are even more expensive than the high-yielding varieties of seeds of the green revolution.

Organic farming, on the other hand, has great potential for farmers like Bahadur and his family. Many small-plot farmers already practice organic farming by necessity if not by choice, because they cannot afford the pesticides and herbicides proscribed by organic farming standards. The problem is the difficulty in implementing systems to certify millions of scattered one-acre organic farms as organic, and to collect and market their produce.

Because of the remarkable success of the green revolution, many poverty eradication leaders are encouraging small-acreage farmers to adopt green revolution seeds and strategies. But for many small-plot farmers, there are less costly and less risky options that would increase the amount of food they grow for the table.

A New Agriculture for Dollar-a-Day One-Acre Farmers

The new agriculture designed to end poverty on small farms needs to be rooted in a thorough understanding of one-acre farms in developing countries and of the daily experiences, hopes, and dreams of the families who earn their livings on them.

The thousands of dollar-a-day one-acre farmers I have interviewed dream of two things:

1. Growing enough to keep their families fed through the year.

2. Earning enough income every year to end their poverty.

GROWING TO KEEP THE FAMILY FED

Prun Chhon and his family live in Tamol village in Cambodia, two hours south of Pnom Penh. He and his family grow rice, rice, and more rice on their one-hectare (2.4 acres) of land. They grow two rice crops each year during the long monsoon season. Chhon estimates that it takes about two tons of rice to feed the twelve people in his family for a year, and they are producing about a ton now from each of their two rice crops. Of course, farmers in Taiwan, Japan, and other countries are producing more than five tons of rice per hectare by using green revolution seeds, much more fertilizer than Chhon applies, and better irrigation. But this requires a much bigger investment in seeds, fertilizer, and chemicals than Chhon and his family can afford, and even if they could borrow the money, they couldn't afford to take the risk of losing such a big investment in a major flood.

Prun Chhon applies urea to his rice fields twice for each crop, broadcasting it by hand. He says his total investment in seed, fertilizer, and chemicals is about fifty-five dollars. Much of the urea washes away in a heavy rain, and some of it gases off. But now he hopes that a new form of sustained-release urea granules introduced by IDE, granules that he and his wife poke into the ground with a stick between every four rice plants, will all go to his plants and double his yield, even though it increases his input costs from fifty-five dollars to seventy-four dollars. If they can double their yield, they could end up producing four tons and selling two, bringing in three hundred to four hundred dollars in income and at the same time feeding the family. But because of the extra cost, Prun Chhon and his wife will try it on only one of their rice crops this year—if it works, they will apply it to both crops next year.

Next to his house, Prun Chhon and his family grow and then eat an eighth of an acre of vegetables. They irrigate this plot by bucket from a stream six hundred feet from the house. Perhaps with IDE's help, they can figure out how to move the water to the field with a treadle pump, deliver it to vegetables with a low-cost drip system, and sell their vegetables at a high price during the dry season. But for now, all they can consider is rice.

It takes about a ton (nine hundred kilograms) of rice to feed the average rural family for a year. But most dollar-a-day farmers produce about seven hundred kilos, only enough to keep the family fed for nine months, and if they can't earn enough through finding work, they go hungry.

Most one-acre farmers put first priority on using their land to keep their families fed through the year. They have at least three choices:

1. Increase the yields of their grain crops by using green revolution seeds and the water and fertilizer they require.

2. Adopt lower-risk strategies such as implanted sustained-release urea granules and the System for Rice Intensification (SRI), which increase grain yields with traditional seeds and low-cash investments.

3. Add five hundred dollars a year in net income by growing high-value, labor-intensive cash crops on a quarter acre, and use it to buy the food they need.

GROWING MORE FOOD WITH GREEN REVOLUTION INPUTS

The green revolution hasn't arrived in Africa yet, and most dollar-a-day small-farm families don't use green revolution seeds and strategies, so they continue to get grain yields of one to three tons per hectare. There are at least three critical barriers to smallholder access to the green revolution. The first is absent access to affordable irrigation. The second is the comparatively high cost of green revolution inputs to cash-strapped dollar-a-day farmers. The third is the unacceptable risk of loss in a ten-year flood or drought.

Without access to dry-season irrigation, small-acreage farmers have to depend on monsoon rains to provide water for their subsistence crops. In Nepal, it's not unusual to have three weeks without rain during the monsoon season, so a dollar-a-day farmer who borrows fifty dollars from a moneylender to adopt high-yielding varieties of rice risks losing his land in four months when it comes time to pay the moneylender one hundred dollars. Another farmer, who invests fifty dollars in high-yielding rice in the monsoon season in Bangladesh, risks losing it all in a ten-year flood.

LOW-COST LOW-RISK STRATEGIES FOR GROWING MORE FOOD

Strategies such as implanted sustained-release urea capsules, which IDE has field-tested and marketed successfully with small-plot farmers in the central hills of Vietnam and in Nepal and Bangladesh, usually cost little more than traditional urea broadcasting, and lower the risk of loss from runoff in heavy rains, while they increase yields by 20 percent or more. If a family's workers produce seven hundred kilos of the nine hundred kilos they need to keep food on the table, and can increase the yield to eight hundred fifty kilos, they only have to find the money to buy fifty kilos instead of two hundred.

The System for Rice Intensification (SRI),[34, 35] a low-cost, more labor-intensive way to increase rice yields, is spreading rapidly among small-plot farmers, although it has generated considerable controversy. Most rice is grown underwater in rice paddies. This keeps rice plants continuously supplied with water and suppresses weeds. Since few dollar-a-day farmers have access to formal irrigation, they depend on monsoon rainfall to provide water to their rice crop. Travelers going south from Kathmandu to the Tarai plains of Nepal behold miles and miles of terraces on slopes so steep they would challenge a mountain goat. Many of these terraces were built several generations ago with hand tools assisted by animal power. Each terrace collects monsoon rainwater, floods a small area planted with rice, and passes it on to the terrace below, all the way down to the foot of the mountain.

In contrast to the usual practice of growing rice, the SRI approach plants rice seedlings farther apart—similar to the way most people grow tomatoes—keeping their roots wet with periodic irrigation. Many tests of this approach report that rice plants grown with this method are sturdier and have a healthier root system, partly because the soil is aerated. Yields as much as double those achieved with the conventional flood method. This gives small-plot farmers the attractive option of increasing their rice yields without changing from their traditional varieties and without risking a big investment in inputs. IDE's initial trials of SRI in Vietnam, Cambodia, and India have produced encouraging results. SRI opens up the possibility of irrigating small rice fields with low-cost sprinkler and drip systems using much more modest water sources. The first field tests in India combining SRI with a low-cost drip-irrigation system have produced promising increases in yield and quality of the rice crop.

GROWING FOR CASH TO BUY FOOD

The third approach to keeping the small-farm family fed holds the most promise in the long run, but often at first appears too risky to small-acreage farmers. They can earn an additional net income of five hundred dollars a year by growing a quarter acre of irrigated high-value cash crops during the dry season, and use the cash from fruits and vegetables to buy the rice, wheat, or corn needed to cover whatever shortfall remains after they have adopted low-cost, low-risk approaches to increasing their yields of staple crops. Millions of farmers have already taken advantage of this entrepreneurial approach.

The Path to New Wealth for Dollar-a-Day One-Acre Farmers

Small farms in developing countries have the lowest labor rates in the world—between five and ten cents an hour. On a level playing field, small farms using family labor consistently outperform big farms using hired labor. The first step that will lead to prosperity for small farms is to identify four or five high-value off-season fruits or vegetables for each agroclimatic zone that are likely to have sustainable market demand and can be grown successfully on quarter-acre intensively cultivated, irrigated plots. Then, for each agroclimatic zone, practical steps are taken to stimulate private-sector networks that open smallholder access to the affordable irrigation, inputs, and skills required to grow these crops, and to the transportation and trading networks required to sell them at a profit. IDE has already helped more than 2.5 million small-farm families dramatically increase their income using this approach.

But to make it available to 800 million dollar-a-day rural people requires a bold new agricultural initiative centered on one-acre farms, an initiative comparable in size to the green revolution itself.

We need to develop species of fruits, vegetables, and other high-value cash crops customized for small plots.

We need to design and disseminate through the private sector a range of affordable small-plot irrigation technologies.

And we need to develop new techniques of crop rotation, pest management, and intensive diversified horticulture for one-acre farms and quarter-acre plots.

Only a tiny proportion of the agricultural research in the world to-day is centered on optimizing net cash income from the quarter-acre plots and one-acre farms where most of the world's poorest people make their livings. Modern agriculture remains preoccupied with green revolution strategies and the contribution that biogenetics can make to improved crop productivity, techniques that are centered on large farms.

There are exceptions—the Asian Vegetable Research and Development Center (AVRDC) focuses on vegetable production that has great relevance for small farms, and some of the institutions in the Consultative Group on International Agricultural Research (CGIAR) are paying more attention to income-generating strategies on small farms.[36] But even when scientists turn their attention to small farms, their major focuses continue to be macroeconomic policies and green revolution practices, instead of starting at the level of the small-plot farmer and working from there. A conference in England on "The Future of Small Farms" in 2005[37] discussed macroeconomic trends, prospects for the adoption of green revolution and biogenetic technologies on small farms, and the impact of the growing supermarket sector on small-farm production, but had little to say that small-acreage farmers themselves would find useful.

Ending the poverty of most of the people in the world who now survive on less than a dollar a day requires the creation of a transformed agriculture that develops labor-intensive cash crops and cultivation methods capable of optimizing income on one-acre farms.

Monsoon Tomatoes: A Paradigm for the Small-Farm Income Revolution?

In most developing countries, tomato prices reach their peak in the monsoon season, when moisture and humidity provide ideal conditions for molds and diseases to thrive. The Asian Vegetable Research and Development Center (AVRDC)[38] developed a profitable approach that allows small farmers to grow tomatoes in the monsoon season, when prices are at their peak.

First, AVRDC grafted tomato cuttings on disease-resistant egg-plant rootstock in the controlled environment of small greenhouses. These seedlings were planted on raised beds under plastic rain shelters that directed the rain to runoff channels between the raised beds. A hormone spray, applied during blossom time, stimulated the blossoms to set. The technique for growing monsoon tomatoes was adapted to conditions in Bangladesh by researchers at the Bangladesh Agriculture Research Center (BARC). Although glitches developed in the commercialization and mass dissemination of this approach in Bangladesh, it holds great promise as a method to increase the income small-acreage farmers can earn from tiny plots by selling their tomatoes at three times the normal price. IDE helped sixty-two small-plot farmers in the hills of Nepal near Pokhara install bamboo-frame plastic rain shelters to grow monsoon tomatoes that were then irrigated by low-cost drip systems. Total installation cost for a fifty-square-meter simple greenhouse plus the drip system was one hundred twenty-five dollars, and farmers earned two hundred dollars a year in net income. If these results are sustainable, an otherwise landless laborer with access to one hundred square meters of land and with credit can earn new income of four hundred dollars a year by growing intensively cultivated monsoon tomatoes, rotated with other high-value crops.

High-Value Crops from the Land of the Landless

I asked the leaders of several villages in rural areas in the hills of Nepal and in western India to introduce me to the two poorest landless families in each village. I was astonished to learn that functional landlessness in rural villages in developing countries is an illusion. Virtually all "landless" families in rural areas in developing countries have functional access to at least one hundred square meters of arable land provided by the landlord or the village commons, if they don't own it themselves. With a three-dollar drip kit, a few seeds, and sometimes some instruction in intensive horticulture and marketing, they can earn some serious money. When I surveyed landless families who did just that, I was amazed at their creativity.

Many used the roofs of their cottages as land-extenders. A woman I interviewed in a tribal village two hours from the town of Indore, India, had three papaya trees in her yard, and two squash vines spreading on the thatched roof of her house. But she grew them only for her family's consumption. It had never occurred to her that she had room for ten papaya trees instead of three and for four squash vines instead of two, and that she could earn new income by selling part of what she produced. The whole family washed in a designated spot in the courtyard, and it would be easy for them to increase their crop yields by throwing their wash water into the gravity bag of a three-dollar drip system. She could start growing bitter gourd vines on the small fence enclosure for her animals. If she learned hand-pollination techniques for the squash blossoms when they appeared on her vines, she could probably double their yield. And she could use manure tea or diluted human urine to fertilize her crop.

Why not invest serious agricultural research into optimizing the diet improvement and income that "landless" families in developing countries can generate from the small patches of land next to their homes and on their rooftops? A logical first step would be a survey of the crops and practices of exemplary landless farmers who are already doing it. This could be followed by the development of research and on-farm test plots, and a contest for the family or agriculture research team that can produce the largest net annual income from a rooftop and a hundred-square-meter plot.

Fertilizers for Small Plots

Most one-acre farmers in developing countries have access to a little cow or buffalo manure, which they apply as top dressing before they plant their crops. Many later apply a little urea to their grain crops, far short of the recommended dose. When they grow vegetables, many don't apply any fertilizer beyond the initial manure top-dressing. Applying affordable fertilizer through the crop cycle would dramatically improve yields and quality.

Small-plot farmers rarely use some attractive options that they have for applying at least a small amount of low-cost fertilizer to their fruits and vegetable plants once a week through the growth cycle. Using these options could double their income.

If they have one or two animals or access to a bit of manure from a neighbor, they can make manure tea. A burlap bag full of manure is immersed in a drum of water and left there for two days. When the bag is pulled out, the drum of water contains a concentrated solution of plant nutrients, which needs to be diluted one to ten with water before it can be applied to plants by hand or, better still, through the gravity tank of a three-dollar drip system that delivers it directly to the roots of plants.

For those with no access to animal manure, a simpler and cheaper method is available. All it takes is for family members to urinate through a funnel into a stoppered container, add five to ten parts water, and apply the mix to plants. Human urine is sterile, except for rare instances of urinary tract infection. An average adult produces more than five hundred kilos (twelve hundred pounds) of urine per year, with a soluble nitrogen content of 12 percent and 3 to 5 percent of soluble potassium and phosphorus. This is the equivalent of twelve hundred pounds of totally soluble 12-4-4 fertilizer a year. Four family members capturing half their urine will collect more than enough to provide the base nutrients for a quarter-acre vegetable plot.

Small-plot farmers learn optimal fertilizer practice rapidly. An IDE staff member with a bicycle became the equivalent of a barefoot agronomist in the hills of Nepal. In a remote village, he provided hands-on instruction to a group of eight women with no prior experience growing vegetables. They mastered advanced fertilizer and micronutrient strategies and became cutting-edge horticulturists in one growing season.

Crop Rotation and Integrated Pest Management on Tiny Patches of Land

Customizing the principles of integrated pest management (IPM) and crop rotation for quarter-acre plots requires a transformation in farming practice, supported by new agricultural research. But although there are challenges in adapting current farming strategies to tiny patches of land, small farms have ready access to useful local information. Small-plot vegetable growers in a hill village in Nepal in 2002 were losing most of their lettuce seedlings to an insect they described as a "stem-cutting cricket." None of the pesticides recommended by the local agri-vet dealer worked. But one of the villagers found a solution that had proved successful a year or two earlier in a neighboring village. The solution was as simple as it was obvious. The growers cut armfuls of long-stemmed grasses and spread them through the lettuce plot. The crickets couldn't distinguish between lettuce stems and grass stems, and crop losses slowed to a manageable trickle.

What is needed is no mystery—a new field of research applying effective crop rotation and integrated pest management strategies to high-value, labor-intensive cash crops grown on the microplots of one-acre farmers in developing countries.

These new income-generating species of cash crops and the cultivation methods to grow them effectively will make it possible for dollar-a-day farmers to earn enough income to move into the middle class. Will farmers leave their land as their income increases? Of course they might. If a farmer's son becomes a doctor in the city, what's wrong with that? If a farmer earns enough money to leave the farm and start a small shop in town, more power to him! If another farmer stays on the farm because he likes it and it's the most effective way to earn a living, great! Prosperity ends hunger and gives farm families the freedom to choose.

Treadling in comfort

Outdoor vegetable market in India

CHAPTER EIGHT

Creating Vibrant New Markets That Serve Poor Customers

BAHADUR AND HIS FAMILY NEEDED ACCESS TO A VILLAGE DEALER to get good cucumber seeds and fertilizer and a low-cost drip system before they could start producing armfuls of fat green cucumbers. When the cucumbers were ready to pick, the family had to determine how and where they could make a good profit from their crop.

They could get the best price by selling directly to customers from a stand in the Mugling market, luckily only twelve kilometers away, but this took a day of time for Padam Maya Magar Thapa, Bahadur's first wife. Or they could sell to hawkers. When we were stopped at an army checkpoint in Mugling, a twelve-year-old girl with patches on her dress gave us a persuasive pitch to buy cucumber slices wrapped in wet paper towels. (We didn't buy.) We learned later that she was one of Bahadur's salespersons.

Other hawkers with wooden pushcarts sell slices of cucumber through the windows of buses at bus stops. While they make a nice margin, hawkers have to eat their loss (literally) in the form of cucumbers left over at the end of the day. The downside of selling to hawkers is that it takes a lot of haggling, and sometimes in the end no deal is struck.

A third option was to sell to wholesalers at the Mugling market at a set price with no haggling. These wholesalers in turn sold from their pickup trucks to stalls along the road or to retailers in Kathmandu. But the wholesale price fluctuated daily and even hourly, so before they brought their cucumbers to Mugling wholesalers, Bahadur's family had to learn what the price was.

In doing all this, Bahadur and his family had become effective marketplace participants.

Small-Acreage Farmers and the Markets Where They Buy and Sell

Everybody in the world participates in markets. Like Bahadur and his family, yak herders in the snowy mountains of Nepal are entrepreneurs who participate in markets. They make an annual trek to the towns and villages of the Tarai plains to trade yak cheese, dried fruits, and handicrafts for the salt they need to survive. They are often bilked in these transactions because they haven't honed their entrepreneurial skills. It would take practice, perhaps trading year round, to become more skilled negotiators.

The small-plot subsistence farmers in Cambodia who buy a bit of ammonium nitrate fertilizer and sell surplus rice when they have a good crop also participate in markets. The two-acre rice farmers in the Gandaki valley in Nepal who live two days from the nearest road and produce a relatively low-quality smoked ginger for the India market participate in markets, but not very skillfully. They could make more money if they had a better understanding of the quality standards of the traders to whom they sell their ginger, and changed their farming and processing practices to better meet these standards.

The tribal villagers in the central hills of Vietnam who have no written language and grow upland rain-fed rice, providing only half of what their families need for the year, are also market participants. They work from daylight to dusk collecting green rattan vines in the forest, and sell them far too cheaply to clever highway traders in order to buy the rice they need. If the villagers knew more about the going price for rattan in town, they might get paid more. If they could learn how to make simple rattan furniture, they might earn much more.

The 10 million farmers in sub-Saharan Africa who carry water in buckets from streams and ponds to their tiny plots of tomatoes and chili peppers and onions that they then carry to the highway to sell to truckers, who in turn carry the vegetables to cities, participate in markets. If these farmers could find a more efficient way to carry water to their crops, they could produce and earn eight times as much as they do now. The twelve hundred potters who live in the slum of Dharavi in Mumbai and make flowerpots and water pots participate in markets. If they could make high-end ceramics and find ways to sell them to prosperous customers, they could earn much more from their craft.

Unfortunately, the markets where dollar-a-day people are buyers and sellers have more holes than a barrel of Swiss cheese. Most markets in developing countries where dollar-a-day people are buyers and sellers are vestigial, or so far away they can't be reached, or don't exist at all. How can dollar-a-day people increase their income if they don't have access to markets where they can buy the tools they need to produce something of value, as well as markets where they can sell what they produce at a profit?

Markets and Entrepreneurs:
The Mother of Symbiotic Relationships

Entrepreneurs create wealth by exploiting inefficiencies in markets, and markets stay efficient by taking advantage of the activities of entrepreneurs. It is the lively, ever-changing dance between markets and entrepreneurs that breathes life into both activities. The annihilation of entrepreneurs in Pol Pot's Cambodia and in Stalin's Soviet Union stunningly demonstrated what happens to markets and nations when entrepreneurs disappear. But there is a profound difference between the interactions of entrepreneurs and markets in affluent countries and those in developing countries. I have succeeded and failed as an entrepreneur in both.

Niche Opportunities in Mature Markets

In the 1990s two friends of mine and I bought a forty-four-unit apartment complex in Riverton, Wyoming. Because of the collapse of the oil and gas business, the area's biggest employer, vacancy rates were 40 percent, and we bought the apartments for half of what they cost to build. Most of Riverton's apartments were unfurnished, because landlords thought this attracted more-reliable tenants with fewer turnovers. But the only jobs bringing new tenants to town were six-month construction projects, and these temporary construction workers wanted furnished units. The garage sales of people who were leaving provided great opportunities to buy good furniture at a decent price, and our newly furnished units quickly brought our vacancy rate to below 10 percent. We sold our apartments two years later at a good profit.

Identifying niches and filling them is the bread and butter of the regular interplay between markets and entrepreneurs. But rare is the stubborn visionary who, like Henry Ford, creates revolutionary new markets.

A Motor Car for the Workingman

When Ford burst on the scene, thirty or forty car companies were producing and selling automobiles for twenty-two hundred dollars or more to rich playboys. Ford's dream was to build a five-hundred-dollar car for the workingman. To reach this goal, he invented the assembly line, broke the monopoly of big car manufacturers, and organized a national network of dealers backed by shrewd marketing and promotion. To get the price down, he cut the weight of cars by a third. One of his quotes on cost cutting became famous: "You can have any color you want in a Model T as long as it's black."

Ford gambled that he and his company could make big profits by going for the high-volume, low-margin market. He turned out to be spectacularly right. In 1991, standing on the shoulders of Henry Ford's breakthroughs, global automobile sales passed 54 million.[39]

Making It Smaller and Cheaper

Akio Norita, the dynamic CEO of Sony, said, "I do not serve markets. I create them!" He proved his point by paying RCA twenty-five thousand dollars for the rights to transistor radios at a time customers for hi-fi systems were true believers in the notion that size counts and were willing to pay one or two thousand dollars for a hi-fi set. In Akio Norita's hands, the initially tinny sound quality of transistor radios quickly improved, and they created a continuing revolution in the radio and entertainment industries.

At a time when mainframe computers filled rooms in universities and cost more than a million dollars, Jobs and Wozniak built a computer that fit on a student's desktop and cost less than five thousand dollars, triggering an information revolution that is still going on.

Revolutionary change in markets is usually based on breakthroughs in affordability and miniaturization, married to innovations in marketing and distribution.

If there are thousands of entrepreneurs exploiting niches, and one or two rare entrepreneurs creating revolutions in mature markets, how does all this play out in the markets in developing countries that serve poor customers?

Typically, when niches open up in developing-country markets, not a single entrepreneur steps up to fill them. Markets that serve poor customers in developing countries offer hundreds of Henry Ford–size opportunities that go begging. Twenty-five years ago, many people told me that if there had been such a big demand for an affordable small-plot irrigation tool, the marketplace would have filled it long ago. But this rarely happens in developing-country markets. Today there is unfilled demand for hundreds of millions of affordable small-plot irrigation tools such as treadle pumps and low-cost drip systems, but the market just sits there, virtually undisturbed by a single disruptive innovation.

Why are the markets in developing countries so inefficient? Why are they allowed to sleep so tranquilly, undisturbed by the entrepreneurs who disrupt affluent markets as a matter of course? Why don't armies of entrepreneurs exploit the thousand opportunities that are available as they do in Western markets?

Below are listed some of the more obvious factors that contribute to the inefficiency of markets in developing countries.

Why Developing-Country Markets Operate So Poorly

LACK OF HOPE

Many people have become so used to being poor that they have lost hope about anything changing. A poor village I visited in a remote area in Maharastra grows only subsistence crops with negligible market value. But twelve kilometers down the road an enterprising farmer pipes water from a well next to a government reservoir to irrigate one hundred acres of tomatoes, and calls at least four different markets every morning on his cell phone to find the best price. I went to meet him with seven farmers from the poor village. He agreed to teach them what he knew, but they were reluctant to take advantage of the opportunity. They listed a litany of obstacles that were real enough, but the farmers seemed to lack enough entrepreneurial spirit to overcome those obstacles.

CLOUDED VISION

Paradoxically, people in poor villages often don't have the eyes to see opportunities under their noses, usually because doing so would require a break with normative cultural expectations.

A woman in a tribal village in India carried water by bucket from the community pump to three papaya trees close to the thorn fence that bordered her yard and to two pumpkin vines growing on the roof of her house. She grew only for her table. She had room for ten or twelve papaya trees around the border of her yard and four pumpkin vines on her roof, and with very little effort, she could earn twenty-five hundred rupees (fifty dollars US) from selling her surplus. When I asked her why she didn't do this, she said she had never thought of it and wouldn't know how to go about selling her crops.

NO INTELLECTUAL-PROPERTY PROTECTION

We learned early on in Bangladesh that if we designed a new tool for small-acreage farmers, one of the best ways to find out if it was any good was to put it on the market. Copies of good products appeared within two weeks. Since good products get copied so quickly, why should innovators invest time and money to develop them?

SUBSIDIES

Subsidies, or the promise of subsidies that never materialize, often inhibit the emergence of promising new markets. Five years after we started mass-marketing treadle pumps in Bangladesh, President Ershad announced around election time that he would provide ten thousand free treadle pumps to farmers in his home district. All private-sector sales in the region stopped immediately and stayed close to zero for a year, until farmers finally realized that only one or two thousand pumps of very poor quality would be delivered. Subsidies of 50 percent for small-farm equipment invariably do more to undercut adoption of new products and methods than to promote it.

CORRUPTION

Many private-sector manufacturers of UNICEF hand pumps have learned that their most efficient investment in marketing and distribution is to bribe one or two government buyers. If you are a businessman in any one of several Asian countries, a ten-thousand-dollar investment in buying your son a government job with lifelong under-the-table payments attached is usually a more reliable way to assure his future than investing in a business he could run that fills an unmet market need.

ISOLATION

The five thousand people who live in the town of Jumla in the hills of Nepal are a twelve-day walk from the nearest road. Although small-plot farmers around Jumla grow outstanding apples, the costs to transport them to market in Kathmandu are prohibitive, and so are the relative costs for basic household supplies, which either come in at high cost on small planes or are carried in on the backs of porters. The isolation of many village dollar-a-day families constrains their ability to interact productively with the urban and peri-urban markets where many of their natural suppliers and customers live and conduct their business.

LACK OF INFORMATION

Many of the small-acreage farmers in the hill areas of Nepal have perfect weather and soil conditions to grow off-season vegetables, but they haven't believed it possible to grow vegetables, weren't familiar with intensive horticulture, and didn't know about or have access to low-cost drip irrigation, which was the only way they could effectively harness the limited amounts of water from small streams that they had available in winter or to harness the surplus available in village piped drinking-water systems. They lacked information about prices and demand in the markets in Pokhara and the Kathmandu valley, where they could sell their crops.

POOR ACCESS TO CREDIT

Most dollar-a-day one-acre farmers lack access to the credit they need in order to buy affordable irrigation tools and agricultural inputs. Micro-credit organizations are likely to open an office in more densely populated areas such as peri-urban neighborhoods, where it is easier to achieve the loan density and higher loan values consistent with organizational economic sustainability. They are much less likely to locate in a remote rural area where the customers for their services are widely dispersed and more likely to need a loan for twenty-five dollars than for one hundred twenty-five dollars. Small enterprises in the rural private-sector supply chain, such as workshops making irrigation equipment or postharvest processing enterprises, often also have a difficult time gaining access to credit.

These are some of the more obvious reasons that markets in developing countries are inefficient. But there is a great deal more to learn about these markets and what keeps them from being effective. It will take a series of field-based research studies of the urban and rural areas where poor people are buyers and sellers to learn why these markets operate so poorly.

Creating New Markets That Serve Poor Customers

The solution is to create new markets that serve poor customers. Hundreds of markets, comparable in size and impact to the mass market for motorcars and computers, are waiting to be discovered. This will require an army of entrepreneurs, ranging from the owners of tiny family-based grassroots enterprises to visionary CEOs of multinational organizations who are willing to make radical changes in the design and delivery of their products and services in order to take advantage of massive virgin opportunities for serving these neglected populations that make up 90 percent of the world's customers.

People who live in slums earn their living by finding low-paying jobs in a staggering array of slum enterprises, from garment sweatshops to pottery shops, to leather tanneries, to factories making sutures for export, to kitchens producing sweets for five-star hotels. The one thing shared by all these enterprises is that the wages slum dwellers earn by working in them are extremely low. If small-plot farmers can take advantage of their low-cost labor to grow labor-intensive, high-value cash crops for the upscale market, why can't slum dwellers become the beneficiaries of outsourcing opportunities? Why can't they take advantage of their low labor rates to produce high-value, high-margin, handmade goods that sell for a much higher price than what these workers now make?

Instead of producing cheap T-shirts and saris for the low end of the market, why can't existing slum garment-making enterprises take advantage of the Internet and good management practices to produce high-quality made-to-measure suits, sports jackets, dresses, and blouses for affluent customers? Why can't the potters of Dharavi produce and sell high-value ceramics instead of cheap water pots and flowerpots that face an onslaught of competition from factory-made plastics? Why can't pharmaceutical multinationals start to manufacture and mass-market lower-priced versions of their most successful brands in countries like India, and make a healthy profit doing so?

Some of this is already beginning to happen. Shops that used to make low-value wooden furniture in Dharavi are now carving elegant wooden doors for Mumbai's wealthy homes. Most of the smelly first-stage tanning tanks for raw hides in Dharavi have relocated, but now leather workshops there are producing fashion purses for the shops of Paris.

There is a parallel process happening for many dollar-a-day people in rural areas.

Creating New Markets for Dollar-a-Day Small-Acreage Farmers

As with their brothers in urban slums, the path to new wealth for small-acreage farmers in developing countries lies in growing and selling high-value, labor-intensive products, such as off-season fruits and vegetables, to customers who can afford to buy them. But doing this requires the creation of new markets capable of bringing them the inputs they need to grow their crops, as well as new value chains capable of bringing their goods to market at reasonable prices.

Creating Private-Sector Supply Chains That Serve Small-Acreage Farmers

When we first started promoting treadle pumps in Bangladesh twenty-three years ago, development experts told us that treadle pumps could never make a significant impact, because they could each irrigate only half an acre of land. One-and-a-half million treadle pumps later, these half-acre pumps were irrigating seven hundred and fifty thousand acres at a fraction of the cost of a conventional dam-and-canal system to accomplish the same thing. There is vast untapped potential in marketing to millions of one-acre farmers. The engine to make this happen is the activation of private-sector supply chains.[40]

In the case of treadle pumps, we created a private-sector supply chain by energizing seventy-five small-scale manufacturers, two thousand or more village dealers, and three thousand well-drillers, all earning a living by making, selling, and installing treadle pumps at an unsubsidized fair market price of twenty-five dollars. Below are the eight practical steps we took to make this happen, steps that were derived from an

A manufacturer of treadle pumps

active learning process about how existing rural markets worked in Bangladesh.

REMOVE SUBSIDIES

Over a period of two years, we persuaded development organizations promoting manual irrigation pumps in Bangladesh to remove most of the subsidies they were providing to help small-plot farmers buy and install treadle pumps.

LOWER THE COST

By providing PVC pipe in place of galvanized iron pipe for tube wells, and giving small-plot farmers the choice of buying treadle pumps at three different quality standards, starting with a low-cost pump with a two-year life span that ended up taking over 55 percent of the market, we gave small-plot farmers trade-off choices in affordability.

RECRUIT SMALL-SCALE MANUFACTURERS

By offering assistance in marketing and meeting quality standards, we recruited four small-volume workshop entrepreneurs who each invested five hundred to two thousand dollars (US) to get into the treadle-pump

A village dealer in
Bangladesh

production business. As marketplace demand for treadle pumps increased, seventy-five small-scale manufacturers entered the market,
most of them with no direct links to IDE.

RECRUIT VILLAGE DEALERS

We recruited village dealers who were already selling items such as
plastic pipe or tools to villagers and who were willing and able to invest
in an inventory of ten treadle pumps. When these dealers were able to
sell twenty-five treadle pumps a year with a margin of 12 percent, they
made enough money to sustain themselves. As demand increased,
more than two thousand village dealers entered the treadle-pump
marketplace.

TRAIN WELL-DRILLERS

We ran a three-day course, offering a diploma, that trained three thousand village well-drillers to drill wells and install treadle pumps without leaks and become promoters for treadle pumps in their villages.

OPEN ACCESS TO MICROCREDIT

We formed a partnership with Grameen Bank, Brac, Proshika, and
other Bangladeshi organizations that made credit available for group

members interested in buying treadle pumps. Grameen Bank alone provided credit that enabled twenty-five thousand of its members to purchase treadle pumps from Grameen dealers. Still, most of the customers for treadle pumps lacked access to microcredit.

IMPLEMENT MARKETING AND PROMOTION INITIATIVES

To bring manufacturers, dealers, and well-drillers to the volume thresholds needed for the product to become profitable, we instituted marketing and promotion campaigns that included:

1. Calendars, leaflets, and posters.

2. Troubadours. We hired traveling four-member bands that composed a song about the treadle pump and performed at farmers markets and fairs, with leaflets directing potential customers to dealers.

3. Drama. We hired a troupe of traveling actors who gave performances in open-air settings of a play specifically written to promote treadle pumps.

At a village market in Bangladesh, troubadours sing a song about treadle pumps.

The plot of this full-length feature movie shown in Bangladesh includes a treadle pump system.

4. A full-length feature movie. We produced a ninety-minute feature movie, using top Bangladeshi male and female leads and a popular director. The treadle pump played a central role in the plot. Using a generator and a screen, the movie played to a rural audience of a million people a year.

ESTABLISH STRATEGICALLY PLACED DEMONSTRATION PLOTS

We established demonstration plots in visible locations where, using treadle pumps, real farmers made money from crops, plots where dealers could bring potential customers to interview successful farmers.

All these steps were taken by a team of Bangladeshi staff whose market-creation activities cost an additional eight dollars for each twenty-five-dollar treadle pump sold. Because of the absence of intellectual-property protection, this marketing cost could not be added to the market price but was covered instead by grants from the Canadian and Swiss governments. These grants provided a market-creation subsidy instead of subsidizing the cost of the individual treadle pump to farmer-purchasers.

The same approach works equally well to create private-sector supply chains delivering seeds, fertilizer, pest-management tools, and other inputs to small farms.

Creating New Markets for the Crops That One-Acre Farmers Grow

After successfully growing enough wheat, rice, or corn to feed themselves for a year, most savvy dollar-a-day farm families are open to turning their attention to producing high-value, off-season cash crops for the market. But which of these crops should they grow?

Deciding What Crops to Grow

Since it is impossible to predict the future market value of any crop, the best way to cut risk and make money consistently is to grow four or five different high-value crops likely to command consistently good prices in the market. The best option is to apply the venture capital approach—if you plant five cash crops, you might feed one to the pigs, break even or better on three, and make a big profit on the fifth.

We use three practical steps to identify the four or five high-value crops we recommend in each agroclimatic zone, a geographic area with similar climate and market conditions with populations from a few hundred thousand to 40 million.

- **Interview fifty exemplary farmers.** Ask them what they made the most money on last year. This quickly identifies fifteen or more potential crops in each area.

- **Do a quick analysis of likely future market demand.** Interview experienced market traders making a living from each of the crops. This weeds out the crops with shallow or widely fluctuating market demand, and narrows down the list to the four or five likely to have sustainable future market demand.

- **Interview regional and government agriculture experts and data banks.** Identify one or two new high-value cash crops that can be added to the list.

In Maharastra, India, for example, pomegranate is one of the crops IDE recommends, because it grows well there and has large unmet market demand in Delhi markets, as well as significant export demand in the Middle East. Baby bananas, eggplant, sweet limes, and off-season vegetables are also recommended crops in Maharastra. Of course, small-plot farmers themselves make the final decision about what to grow. Since the optimal crop pattern changes each year, the important thing for farmers is to learn how to select the best high-value crop pattern themselves, which requires that they become committed students of trends in market demand as well as growing conditions.

Dismantling the Transport Barrier

Zambia provides a Keystone Kops example of how to undercut short-haul private-sector transport enterprises. Several years ago, the government implemented a free transport system that promptly put small rural transport enterprises out of business. This initiative collapsed because the funding ran out, and an epidemic of ridge disease of cattle put thousands of farmer-owned bullock carts out of action. When I visited in 2003, one-acre farmers I interviewed were paying a third of what they got for their vegetables just to transport them a few kilometers to the nearest road, where they could contract with a trucker to carry them to a city market.

The answer for many large development donors is to build more roads. But you can wait a very long time in many places before a road is built to reach your remote village. Of course, there are much less expensive options that can be implemented while a village waits for a road to be built. Chinese rototillers pulling trailers with thousand-kilo loads up and down hills in Kathmandu can operate on very rough terrain. Donkey cart entrepreneurs make good money hauling all kinds of loads in Somalia and Tanzania. Thousands of rickshaw vans, each pulling a platform trailer instead of a passenger seat, ply their trade all over Bangladesh. It would be relatively inexpensive to implement a project in rural Zambia setting up five entrepreneurs with motorcycle trailers, five with Chinese rototiller trailers, five with donkey carts, and five with rickshaw vans, see which ones become profitable, and then help them spread. Yet I have never been able to find a development donor willing to support this.

Making Mountains Out of Molehills

For a supermarket supplier in Africa, it is much easier to make one stop at a thousand-acre farm to pick up vegetables and to hold one farmer accountable for meeting quality standards than it is to make a thousand stops at one-acre farms. Unless one-acre farmers come up with an effective group collection and quality-control strategy, they lose out to large-farm competitors.

The owner of a thousand-acre private coffee plantation in Zambia, whose coffee-processing machinery was underutilized, contracted with forty-five two-acre farmers to process and market their coffee, improving both his income and theirs. If they have business-savvy managers, farmer co-ops often can carry out the same functions.

Adding Value Close to the Farm

Since the beginning of time, farmers have complained they don't get paid enough. "Look," they say. "It took me four months to grow this plastic bag full of tomatoes, and I sold it yesterday for fifty cents. Today I see that same bag of tomatoes for sale in the supermarket for two dollars. How come I get fifty cents for four months' work, and the supermarket gets a dollar fifty in one day?"

That farmer can capture some of that dollar fifty if he can do a little value-added processing, or if he can leapfrog over one or two middlemen.

Sometimes small decentralized farm-level processing can be more efficient than the large city-based processing plants, in spite of the dogma of the economy of scale put forth by many economists. Central planners in the Soviet Union realized that the construction costs for grain silos per kilo of stored grain drop as silos get bigger, so they built huge silos. They forgot that during the time of the wheat harvest, it rained so much that most roads were impassable, and fewer large silos meant longer transport hauls. The outcome of building huge silos was that huge piles of grain were left lying in the fields to rot in the rain. In the same way, small added-value village-based processing plants are often more cost-effective than large city-based plants, leave more money in the hands of the poor farmers who grow the crops to be processed, provide new jobs for poor people in the village, and create positive multiplier effects from money that circulates through the village economy.

Half of the Brazil nuts gathered from standing rain forests by rubber tappers in Brazil spoil during the moist two-week barge ride down to large processing plants in Belem at the mouth of the Amazon River. In partnership with the rubber tappers co-op, IDE designed a way to dry, shell, and package Brazil nuts at the rain forest gathering point. By removing the shells, the decreased spoilage and 75 percent decrease in transport weight more than made up for the economies of scale of the larger city plants. Partnering with Cultural Survival, a Boston organization of anthropologists who brokered the sale of the nuts processed in the village to Ben and Jerry's in Boston, provided the rubber tappers with a better price. Processing at the village provided new employment opportunities for the families of rubber tappers, increased the income rubber tappers received from gathering nuts, and helped preserve the rain forest because it empowered the rubber tappers who were the most effective protagonists for keeping the rain forest standing.

There are hundreds of opportunities for adding value at the village level. Farmers in Zambia grow red paprika, dry it, and sell it to middlemen who truck it and sell it to large plants in South Africa, where essential oils containing red vegetable dyes are extracted and sold for premium prices in Europe. From the frankincense and myrrh of biblical times to lavender and lemongrass, large city-based plants extract essential oils from crops that can be grown on small farms and sold at huge markups as ingredients for perfumes and cosmetics, or in half-ounce vials going for six dollars and up to aroma-therapy practitioners. The centuries-old way to extract essential oils is steam distillation, the same process bootleggers have always used to make moonshine. It is entirely feasible to design small, efficient, village-based steam distillation units that sell for fifteen hundred dollars, or five thousand dollars for bigger ones. This would address both the aggregation and quality-control problems often faced by small-farm producers, create a network of new village-based enterprises, and put more money in the pockets of small-farm grassroots enterprises. If a network of small, village-based steam distillation units for paprika sprang up in Zambia, it would change all the economics of the current paprika industry in that country.

It is possible and practical for every poor village in a developing country to make a list of the crops produced in the area that have the greatest economic value, and the processing applied to them that adds most value. For each of these crops, a rapid initial business plan will identify promising niche opportunities where value-added processing in the village can be competitive in the marketplace, much as was the village processing of Brazil nuts. But this requires what most people experience as a counterintuitive design process that puts affordability, small size, and adding value at the village level first, and that looks for marketplace opportunities to be competitive with large, centralized city plants.

An increasing number of development organizations are demonstrating that creating new markets to increase the income of the rural poor is both practical and feasible.

TechnoServe Creates New Markets for Pineapple Growers in Ghana

TechnoServe, a Connecticut-based international development organization that creates new markets to alleviate poverty, implemented a program to improve pineapple farmers' quality and production volume in Ghana,[41] where small-acreage farmers together produce 62,200 tons of pineapple a year. This initiative connected the many small-plot farmers of organic pineapples to local, regional, and international markets to increase the incomes of the farmers and of entire communities.

Responding to a request in 2002 by Athena Foods—a company in Ghana that processes pineapples, citrus juices, and concentrates for local and export markets—TechnoServe quickly linked Athena to 311 small-scale organic pineapple and citrus growers, and trained them to meet international quality standards and to produce the documentation needed to get organic certification. By the end of the first year, Athena had purchased three hundred seventy metric tons of oranges and pineapples from these farmers, and sold $398,000 worth of organic juice, earning $300 for each of the farmers.[42] In 2003 TechnoServe helped Athena obtain a $300,000 loan to produce and sell organic juice in Europe and the United States worth $1,059,170. This increased the income of 322 small-scale farmers by an average of $1,162 in a country where average per capita income is $290.

Creating new markets that serve poor customers increases the incomes of poor people by producing and marketing their high-value, labor-intensive products and services. And the new markets have further beneficial results. They have transformative potential in such diverse areas as health, education, transport, and housing.

Give Me a Market So I Can See

According to the World Health Organization, there are 1 billion people in the world who need glasses but don't have them now. Eyeglasses for nearsightedness or farsightedness would correct the vision problems of 70 to 90 percent of these people. For a tailor in a hill village in Nepal who no longer can see to sew, a pair of affordable eyeglasses makes the difference between earning a living and becoming a beggar.

Usually beginning in their forties, many people become unable to focus their vision on near objects, a condition called *presbyopia*. Today you can go into a drugstore in Denver or Amsterdam and select an eight-dollar pair of reading glasses that will correct your vision problem. Why not make a robust version of this display stand available to the 1 billion or so poor people in the world who need eyeglasses?

Adaptive Eye Care, a UK-based company, uses the invention of an Oxford physics professor, Joshua Silver, to bring self-adjusting eyeglasses to people who need them.[43] The constraint here is the cost—fifteen dollars now, perhaps ten dollars or less with volume, but still not affordable to people who earn less than a dollar a day.

New Eyes for the Needy, a US-based organization, shipped three hundred fifty-five thousand donated used eyeglasses in good condition during 2005–2006 to medical missions and charitable organizations in developing countries.[44] The problem here is that giving glasses away is not a scheme that can be scaled up to reach more than a tiny fraction of the 1 billion people who need them.

In the last five years, New York–based Scojo Foundation and its partners have sold fifty thousand reading glasses, at prices from three to five dollars, in India, Bangladesh, and El Salvador, and have referred seventy thousand people to eye-care professionals through a network of six hundred vision entrepreneurs, twenty-six franchise partners, and a number of urban wholesalers distributing to pharmacies and other retail outlets. They hope to sell a million more in the next five years. Graham Macmillan, the executive director of Scojo, tells me that a surprising number of small-acreage farmers are enthusiastic customers for affordable eyeglasses, because without these glasses they can't read the labels on seed packages. Some of them don't know what crop they are planting until it begins to come up.[45]

The combined efforts of Scojo, New Eyes for the Needy, and Adaptive Eyecare have reached less than 1 percent of the 1 billion poor people who need eyeglasses. The rest live with serious visual problems, paying a significant price in lost income because they can't see straight. This is outrageous, because there is such a simple solution in taking advantage of uncomplicated eyeglass display stands that already sell affordable eyeglasses to millions of wealthier customers.

It would take five to ten million dollars in venture capital to start an international company that would buy a million eyeglasses in mainland China at around fifty cents apiece, design robust, visually appealing mobile display stands pushed by people or pulled by bicycles or motor scooters in poor areas, perhaps forming partnerships with major corporations such as Tata in India, developing an effective global distribution and marketing strategy. The company's goal would be to reach sales of fifty million two-dollar eyeglasses within five years, and make a healthy profit doing it.

One-acre dollar-a-day farmers and their urban brothers and sisters are already hard-nosed, stubborn survivalist entrepreneurs ready to take advantage of marketplace opportunities if the price is right, the return is high, and the risk is low. But they need private-sector supply chains to furnish them with the tools, materials, and information required to create high-value products, and private-sector value chains that sell what they produce at an attractive profit. As their incomes increase, they become customers for products like affordable eyeglasses, houses, solar lighting, health care, and education. New markets that serve poor customers will provide opportunities for hundreds of millions of dollar-a-day people to move out of poverty. But a revolution in design is needed to create the range of new income-generating tools that will make this move possible.

A slum is a beehive of grassroots enterprises.

CHAPTER NINE

Slums:
The Incubator
for New Income
Opportunities

WHEN HE WAS EIGHTEEN, DROUGHT RAVAGED HIS VILLAGE, SO Samsuddin traveled from Tirukoyoor in Tamil Nadu to his uncle's home in Bombay. He expected to arrive at a house in the big city, but found himself instead in the middle of a swamp in a slum called Dharavi.[46] Like so many others who migrate from the village, he was looking for a job so he could survive. He found one in his uncle's rice-smuggling business. There was a tax on grain brought into Bombay from outside the city limits, so every morning, Samsuddin, his uncle Hassain, and his three cousins traveled out of the city, bought as much rice as they could carry, at a cost of one rupee and fourteen annas per pound, and hauled it through the swamp to sell at Kalyanwadi for ten rupees per pound.

These are healthy margins. If each of the smugglers carried twenty-five pounds a day, this little enterprise was bringing in the equivalent of twenty-five dollars a day at the rupee exchange rate of the 1950s, a significant amount. His uncle probably didn't pay him much, but food and a place to sleep meant everything to Samsuddin.

When Hassain moved back to their village and his three sons immigrated to Pakistan in 1954–55, Samsuddin found a job at a coal company that paid him a rupee-and-a-half per day. After two years he got a better job at a printing press that paid him fifty-six rupees a month, double his previous salary. He married and moved with his wife into an illegal hut with no electricity or water that they shared with another family.

Then he bought a legal room measuring ten feet by eighteen feet for four hundred seventy-five rupees. One day he met Hamid, a man who knew how to make a popular sweet dessert called *chiki*, helped him find space to produce it, and agreed to take it to shops and sell it. He soon found he could earn twenty-five rupees a day selling chiki, and quit his regular job. Eventually Samsuddin and his wife learned how to make chiki themselves, and when Hamid moved to Calcutta, they took over the business. They made chiki all day, wrapped it in old newspapers, and Samsuddin sold it in cinema halls until eleven at night.

The couple named their product A-1 Chiki, creatively borrowing the name from a popular brand of chewing gum, and the business took off. Now in two gloomy rooms, twenty workers produce A-1 Chiki managed by one of Samsuddin's previous workers, who pays Samsuddin an ongoing royalty. At the age of seventy, Samsuddin lives in Nagri Apartments, a high-rise in Dharavi. He has a plush living room, two phones, a TV set, and curios in a glass cabinet. His two sons are educated and run their own businesses.

Dharavi is the biggest slum in Asia, covering about four hundred fifty acres. Nobody knows exactly how many people live in Dharavi—estimates range from 1 to 5 million. There are many amazing success stories like Samsuddin's in Dharavi, but most of the poor people who come there from rural villages have to scramble to find jobs and barely earn enough to survive. Samsuddin's story illustrates the spirit of enterprise that creates the jobs in slums all over the world that people streaming in from rural villages are seeking.

Krishna Bahadur Thapa and Samsuddin might have been twins. If Bahadur's father had lost his farm when Bahadur was a teenager, Bahadur would probably have had to go to Kathmandu looking for a way to survive on the streets. And if Samsuddin hadn't been fortunate enough to have an uncle who could provide both shelter and a job, he would have been likely to end up living on the sidewalk in Bombay instead of in a hut in the slum, and like many pavement dwellers, he would have stayed there for a long time.

Census takers in developing countries don't count pavement dwellers. SPARC, an NGO organized by slum dwellers, carried out the first census of pavement dwellers in Mumbai in 1985. In the Byculla area alone, this census enumerated six thousand households, accounting for nearly twenty-seven thousand pavement dwellers.[47]

Zenia Tata, a colleague of mine at IDE, grew up in Bombay, now known as Mumbai, where her parents have lived in a third-story flat for thirty years. She told me the story of a pavement-dwelling family she and her parents have known for twenty-five years, because they live on the sidewalk below her parents' balcony. The mother and father in this sidewalk family are both lame, crippled by polio, and they live with their healthy five-year-old son on a spot originally settled by the husband's parents. The husband makes a living darting in and out of the heavy traffic of the street next to the sidewalk where they live, washing car windshields for twenty-five paisa (about half a US penny). He also occasionally washes taxis at a taxi stand down the street. His wife, who gets around on two crutches, earns money stringing and selling marigold garlands.

The couple and their child live with no shelter. When it rains hard in the monsoon season, they move to a nearby park where they attach a tarpaulin to a fence and weight the sides down with rocks. Each morning, they and other sidewalk dwellers lift a heavy steel manhole cover above a major city water-delivery channel, and members of the entire community of pavement dwellers lift water by rope and bucket for an hour or two. The parents in this family go to the toilet in a public lavatory in the park, but their five-year-old son squats down in the gutter next to their sidewalk home and defecates there, with the encouragement of his mother. At his age, it may be too difficult to train him to use the toilet in the park.

Until now, IDE and I have focused on rural poverty. But it seems to me that slum dwellers can increase their access to jobs and income by making and marketing labor-intensive, high-value products, just like their small-acreage-farm brothers.

For centuries, the rural poor have been flocking to cities to find jobs when their crops fail in times of flood and drought or, worse still, when they lose their farms. Many move back to their home village if jobs become available there. If millions of dollar-a-day farmers find ways to increase their income as Bahadur and his family did, current projections that 2 billion more people will live in the world's cities by the year 2030[48] will have to be radically altered.

Slums and poor rural areas have one more important thing in common. Slums have even more grassroots enterprises of all shapes and sizes where poor people can find work and income than do most poor rural areas. This array of large and small enterprises provides the jobs that attract poor people who can no longer survive in their villages. Many of them operate on the edge of legality or beyond the edge.

During India's prohibition period, Dharavi was home to large, powerful, lucrative bootlegging operations, complete with fleets of delivery vehicles operating under the helpful supervision of police partners. Identify a popular brand of luxury soap in India, and you will find a copycat version for sale in Dharavi at one-fifth the price. Multinational organizations work through jobbers to have their empty plastic barrels—previously filled with anything from cooking oil to corrosive chemicals—inspected, cleaned, and returned for re-use. The fact that some of them contained chemicals that could cause serious health problems for slum-dwellers cleaning them seems unimportant; if workers object, they are easily replaced. Like illegal immigrant marketplaces for migrant workers in the United States, under-the-table enterprises in Dharavi play a vital role in the Indian economy.

Every square inch of Dharavi is used for some productive activity.[49] A rough calculation made by residents estimates the money turned over in Dharavi every day to be about 50 million rupees (about a million dollars). A 1986 survey carried out by the National Slum Dwellers Federation identified 1,044 manufacturing operations, and many smaller operations in homes and lofts weren't counted.

The survey reported 244 small-scale manufacturers, employing five to ten people, and 43 big industries, including an international company making sutures for Western markets and a large factory making copies of a popular brand of toothpaste. Also identified were 152 businesses making food products, some of which were served in Mumbai's five-star restaurants, 111 restaurants, 722 scrap-and-recycling units, 85 enterprises making products for export, and 25 bakeries. The large tanneries with their foul-smelling processes have for the most part moved out of Dharavi, but people who make export leather goods remain and opium dens still operate. Grassroots enterprises operate in slums without having to pay much attention to child-labor laws or job-safety regulations.

The grassroots enterprises in slums around the world where slum-dwellers earn their livings—dubbed "informal sector enterprises" by UN and government officials—operate without licenses, pay no taxes, and appear and disappear like puffs of smoke, yet they fill important needs not met by the formal sector. In every city in developing countries, unlicensed itinerant hawkers who live in squatters shacks in the slums sell a panoply of goods and services: sweets, steaming meals, bananas, T-shirts, flowers, household goods, haircuts, trinkets, and laundry services. Like migrant laborers from Mexico in the United States and bootleggers in times of prohibition, these unlicensed grassroots enterprises often survive *because* they operate below the regulatory line, not in spite of doing so.

Slums not only provide jobs from the informal enterprises that operate within them. They also provide low-cost housing close to menial jobs that may be available in the city. Because people live so much closer together in slums, it is easier to collect products like home-stitched garments from slum residents than it is to collect vegetables from scattered farms.

The growth of slums like Dharavi in the last fifteen years has been unprecedented. In 1990 there were nearly 715 million slum dwellers in the world. By 2000 the slum population had increased to 912 million and it is approximately 998 million today. People who live in slums represent 43 percent of the urban population in developing regions. UN-HABITAT[50] estimates that if current trends continue, the slum population will reach 1.4 billion by 2020. Not all slum dwellers and pavement dwellers earn less than a dollar a day, but probably close to between 300 and 400 million people living in slums and on pavements do survive on less than a dollar a day.

Of Nairobi's 2.3 million residents, 1.4 million live in more than one hundred slum and squatter communities scattered through the city and on its fringes, occupying 5 percent of the city's residential land. Sub-Saharan Africa hosts the largest proportion of the urban population living in slums (71.9 percent); 166 million out of a total urban population of 231 million are classified as slum dwellers.[51]

The informal sector plays an important role not only in cities but also in the national economies of developing countries. In Africa the informal sector accounts for about 20 percent of GDP and employs about 60 percent of the urban labor force. In the Philippines, it accounts for 36 percent of employment in urban areas, and in Dhaka, Bangladesh, 63 percent. The informal sector provides between 60 and 67 percent of all employment in Guatemala, El Salvador, Honduras, Costa Rica, and Nicaragua.[52]

Opportunities for Slum Dwellers and Pavement Dwellers to Move Out of Poverty

The UN's Millennium Project Task Force on Improving the Lives of Slum Dwellers put first priority on providing improved housing, health care, education, transport, and access to drinking water and toilets. The task force estimates that these improvements in health, education, housing, and infrastructure for 100 million slum dwellers will cost close to 70 billion dollars over fifteen years.[53] While the task force report recognizes the importance of jobs and the informal enterprises and home-based businesses that provide them, it has little to offer in the form of new action plans to increase and improve the pay level of the jobs they provide.

All these things are important, but if there isn't enough money to address all of them at the same time, what is a reasonable approach to setting priorities? If the slum dwellers were in charge of improving slum conditions, what priorities would they set?

The fact that poor people flock to slums and continue living in them makes the clearest statement of what their priorities are. Why do slum dwellers tolerate sharing one filthy toilet with eight hundred people, walking for half an hour to get a container full of drinking water, and living in overcrowded primitive huts? All things considered, if they were totally destitute with no source of income, they would probably have a better chance of surviving in their home villages than in the slums.

The answer is simple. They live in slums and on sidewalks without a roof if they must because they need jobs and income to survive, and they have made a rational decision that they are more likely to find them in the city than in their villages. There are thousands of informal grassroots enterprises that thrive in slums and need workers. Even if the pay is miserable, it's better than earning nothing, allowing you to survive and keeping open the chance that your life will change just as Samsuddin's did.

This fact that jobs and income are the main inducement for people to live in slums seems to have made little impact on the actions of most of the organizations devoted to improving the lives of slum dwellers. They see the overwhelming needs in water, sanitation, housing, education, and health, and focus their efforts on providing the missing services. The UN Task Force on Improving the Lives of Slum Dwellers focuses on initiatives to alleviate the terrible conditions of housing, insecurity of tenure, water, and sanitation in slums, and to provide critical services such as health and education, but says little or nothing about how to improve the business models, marketing methods, and bottom-line profitability that are critical to the survival and well-being of slum dwellers. But if more jobs and higher wages are so important to the slum dwellers themselves, doesn't it make sense to put priority on increasing the jobs available to them and increasing the income they can earn by improving the profitability of their small businesses?

The direction in which all this leads is not startling. The most important priority for slum dwellers is to increase the income they earn from operating or working in slum-based grassroots enterprises. The most direct path to more jobs and increased income for slum and pavement dwellers is to help the grassroots enterprises where they earn their livings to expand the markets for their products and services and thus increase their profitability.

The first step is to identify how slum enterprises can compete effectively in the global marketplace. This, too, is no surprise. Like their small-farm-enterprise brothers, because these slum-dwelling entrepreneurs can take advantage of having access to the lowest labor rates in the world, they can legitimately lay claim to the title of "the mother of outsourcing."

Slum pottery enterprises in Dharavi provide a good example. Forty-five-year-old Janjibhai M. Kamalia is an active member of

Kumbharwada, a community of potters in Dharavi. He has lived there for forty years and plans to stay. He lives with his wife and three children in a loft overlooking his workshop, while his brother stays with his family on the ground floor, which also has a storage space for the family's pots.[54] Their living and work spaces total four hundred square feet. Janjibhai gets up at dawn and makes pots, and has workers who help him fire up the brick kilns where he bakes his pots later in the day. In the late afternoon, he carries his pots to customers in Mumbai. He makes and sells flowerpots and water jugs. Ismaelbhai and his son operate another small pottery business in Dharavi. After about four hours of work every morning, they fire one hundred large garden pots and sell them at a very low price to a trader.

Twelve hundred families from Gujarat live in Kumbharwada, and more than eight hundred of them earn their living by using traditional potter's wheels to produce ordinary clay water jugs and flowerpots and firing their pots in brick kilns that burn everything from wood to tires, creating a terrific stink. Most of these potters earn less than a dollar a day, although some of the more talented pottery entrepreneurs earn four or five dollars a day and have children with college degrees and good jobs. Could creating new markets end the poverty of Janjibhai Kamalia and the potters who are his neighbors?

In the summer of 2006 my wife and I enjoyed looking at the attractive displays of Roman and Etruscan pots at the Legion of Honor Museum in San Francisco. I was surprised to see replicas of them for sale in the museum gift shop at prices ranging from twenty-five to two hundred dollars.

Why couldn't the potters of Dharavi be trained to create handmade replicas of Roman and Etruscan pots, and get the help from experienced entrepreneurs to establish a marketing and distribution network through museum gift shops? Would it be possible to sell some of these handsome handmade replicas on the Internet, each with a hand-lettered story about the craftsman in a slum who made it? Wouldn't this eventually provide a much better return on the low-cost labor of slum potters than selling water jugs and flowerpots at the low end of the market, where they encounter competition from mass-manufactured plastic pots?

Could a savvy entrepreneur with connections to museums start a business contracting with potters in Dharavi and other slums all over the world to make handcrafted replicas of museum pieces? I talked with Ron Riverce, from an organization called Potters for Peace, and he said he already knows how the replicas can be fabricated and how to train slum potters to do it.

The same process would apply to designing, producing, and marketing a variety of other high-value handcrafted ceramic products after a careful analysis of market demand, using approaches such as subsector analysis.[55]

That such an approach to pottery is more than a pipe dream has already been demonstrated by Leeia Borda, who visited a slum in Jaipur, India, in 1977 and started a process training slum potters to make new designs of blue pottery, a craft with Turko-Persian origins that now has become a distinctive Jaipur product line distributed by Neerja International, the company Leeia Borda and her partners started. Working with Paul Comar, a French buyer, Leeia has developed hundreds of new products that serve as utility items but retain the identity of the blue pottery craft. Neerja International employs more than one hundred fifty potters.

Of course, I'm just using the example of the potter communities present in most slums to make my point, but there are thousands of other examples. Instead of making shirts and saris to sell to the low end of the market, why couldn't garment-making enterprises in slums connect to an international enterprise that sells high-quality made-to-measure suits, dresses, and shirts to prosperous customers in Europe and the United States and Japan, complete with three-dimensional realistic images of how the garment looks on the customer, created from a photograph relayed on the Internet? Why couldn't this be done for slum-made products such as fashion leather purses, belts and belt buckles, and custom-made shoes?

This, of course, would require implementing the same basic steps required to make any enterprise successful, the same basic steps that millions of dollar-a-day farmers are now using to move out of poverty.

1. Creating private-sector supply chains to provide reasonably priced materials, tools, designs, and training for slum enterprises producing handmade replicas of museum pottery, or fine silk

scarves or purses for Paris, or hand-carved doors, or the myriad of other high-value, labor-intensive products that could be fabricated by slum residents.

2. Creating private-sector value chains that market the products made by slum residents and that ensure that quality standards are met.

3. Access to credit.

4. Access to prosperous customers able and willing to purchase the high-value products and services produced by slum workers.

If Dharavi's potters could triple their income over a three-year period with such a strategy, they would improve both their housing and their access to water and sanitation. This would not eliminate the need to improve the basic infrastructure and the housing security of slum dwellers. But it would make an important start—one led by the rapidly increasing economic power of the slum dwellers themselves.

This is not a pipe dream; it is already beginning to happen. Dharavi's wood-carvers, for instance, are now employed making high-end carved wooden doors for the rich. Residents of Paraisopolis, the second-largest shanty town in Sao Paulo, Brazil, are changing their lives by recycling jeans and patches of cloth for Recicla Jeans, a venture that employs thirty women. Nadia Rubio Bachi, who started Recicla Jeans, participated in a fashion show in Madrid, and now the company is exporting its fashion products to Lebanon, Portugal, Spain, and Italy.[56]

Does this sound familiar? Development institutions have been encouraging the 800 million people who earn their living from grassroots enterprises centered on one-acre farms to improve their yields of rice, wheat, corn, and other subsistence crops. While they put high priority on growing enough to eat, these one-acre farm families will never create enough wealth to move themselves out of poverty by selling their surplus rice, wheat, and corn, which has relatively low value in the marketplace. But they can earn new income of at least five hundred dollars a year by growing nonmechanized, high-value, off-season crops such as fruits, vegetables, and herbs.

Exactly the same kind of process is applicable to improve the incomes that slum dwellers can earn from working in slum-based enterprises.

Some activities following this process are already going on. To expand rapidly and scale them into a flood of wealth-creating business opportunities, a new movement is needed to harness the energy of successful business leaders motivated to make a difference in the world, and of corporations familiar with the demands of high-end markets and the ways to gain access to them. We need nothing less than a new generation of successful enterprises linking the low-cost labor of the residents of slums to the high-end markets of the world where they can sell their products and services at a reasonable profit.

This will not cure the terrible conditions in housing, sanitation, and water with which slum residents must deal every day. But it will give these people new economic power to take action to transform the slum conditions and to join hands with constructive movements initiated by international businesses, donors, governments, and grassroots NGOs, all taking action to improve the lives of slum dwellers.

Change one person and you can change the world.

CHAPTER TEN

Poverty and the Planet

WHEN KRISHNA BAHADUR THAPA AND HIS FAMILY WERE ABLE to earn five hundred dollars a year in new income, and then a thousand dollars a year, they invested in improvements in their nutrition, health, housing, education, and agriculture—the very things the lack of which many development experts regard as the root causes of poverty. For example, although Padam Magar and Sumitra Magar, Bahadur's two wives, are still illiterate, both their sons finished high school, and the four grandchildren in the family will continue going to school as long as they want to. His family has built an excellent new two-story house, which cost twenty-one hundred dollars US and includes a cement rice-storage bin. They have bought a little over half an acre of land, where they are growing oranges, have expanded their irrigated winter-vegetable production to one acre, and have invested in cattle, buffalo, goats, and tilapia fingerlings.

This is the typical pattern for most small-acreage farmers when they are able to increase their income. They invest in many of the things development experts believe are important, but they do it following their own family's priorities. Because they are now in a better position to pay for things such as school uniforms and medicines, they are able to make better use of publicly funded services such as health clinics and schools. With the increased influence that comes with more money, they are better able to insist to the powers that be that the village school needs a teacher who can read and write, and that a nearby clinic needs to be stocked with enough medicines to keep it from running out after a month or two.

Poverty and the Planet

Ending poverty is probably the most important first step to restore nature's balance on the planet. Each person on earth probably has a different list of the major challenges our planet will face over the next fifty years.

- **If climate change triggered by carbon emissions is at the top of your list,** consider the impact of population growth on carbon emissions and the impact of extreme poverty on population growth. Each of the 3 billion new people on earth by the year 2050 will need food to eat, and energy to run the tractors and the irrigation pumps to produce the food and to power the transport system that carries it to market. Virtually all of these 3 billion new people will be located in poor, developing countries where population growth rates are highest, with sub-Saharan Africa at the top of the list.

  One of the main reasons that population growth rates are high in the rural areas of developing countries is that big families have survival value for small-acreage farmers. A one-acre-farm family in Bangladesh needs three sons to get ahead—one to help with the farm, one to get a good enough education to land a government job capable of supporting the family from small bribes, and one to get a local job that pays enough to keep his brother, the one aiming for a government job, in school. But to end up with three sons means having eight babies, two of which are likely to die before the age of five, leaving three boys and three girls.

If we could bring 600 million dollar-a-day people out of poverty by the year 2020, global population would probably stabilize at around 7 billion instead of the 9 billion we are projecting now, and carbon emissions would drop precipitously.

- **If loss of biodiversity is at the top of your list,** consider the fact that most of the planet's biodiversity is concentrated in the twenty-one key regions of the world where environmentalists are focusing their efforts to create nature preserves. But the species environmentalists are trying to protect are being hunted and eaten by poor people who live around and in the newly created nature preserves. Providing attractive income-generating, poverty-ending alternatives to the need of these people to hunt is one of the most effective practical strategies for maintaining biodiversity on the planet.

- **If you believe the global pandemic of HIV/AIDS, malaria, TB, and other major illnesses is one of the biggest challenges to a viable future for the planet,** consider the evidence that poverty is the single greatest contributor to bad health. Numerous studies have reported a high correlation between poverty and the incidence and prevalence of a range of mental and physical illnesses.[57] Exposure to frequent major life crises such as the death of a loved one or the loss of an important job makes illness rates climb,[58] and poor people experience many more severe life crises than do people with more income. Millions of extremely poor people in Africa have malaria, tuberculosis, or HIV/AIDS and don't have the money to get properly diagnosed or to pay for appropriate treatment. The anguish I heard in the voice of an Indian village widower with three young children after his wife died from pneumonia when he couldn't afford to buy medicine is, unfortunately, not at all rare. I recognized twenty-five years ago that the most important contribution I could make to improved health is to find practical ways to end poverty. This was an important factor leading me to found IDE.

- **If you think the major challenge we face is to provide equitable access to education,** consider the fact that poor people have consistently much lower levels of education than people who are well off. Extremely poor people in rural areas in developing countries need their children at home to help with the farm, and lack money to pay for books, school uniforms, and modest tuition fees.

Poverty is profoundly linked to the major challenges faced by planet Earth over the next fifty years, and to the forces destabilizing nature's balance.

It is clear that public funds are needed to address many of these problems. But if we are successful in eradicating poverty, what contribution are poor people likely to make to the solution of the major challenges that face the planet?

Small-Farm Prosperity Meets Global Warming, Population Growth, Biodiversity, Health, and Education

The newfound wealth of Krishna Bahadur Thapa's family leaves a gentle carbon footprint on the planet. The water they use to irrigate their crops flows by gravity through pipes to their crops. They grow virtually all the food they eat, eliminating the energy consumption required to transport food to them. Some of this energy saving is neutralized by their increased use of chemical fertilizer, which requires energy to produce and to transport to the farm. The drip and sprinkler irrigation systems they use to deliver water to their crops make the most efficient use of their limited water resource. They carry their crops on their backs the short distance to the village collection center, where buyers transport it with reasonable efficiency in small truckloads. They have installed a more efficient cook stove, and they now have electric lights and a small TV set, increasing their energy consumption slightly. The distance from the field to the table, and from their buffalos to the market for their milk, is admirably short.

When most of the families in a very poor village become more prosperous, their collective action and influence begin to be felt in positive ways. When thirty families in a village keep their children in school longer, pay modest tuition fees, and begin to pay some taxes, they are inclined to push to hire a better-prepared teacher, and the quality of education for their children will likely improve.

Smallholder Prosperity and Food Security

Poor families with new income routinely invest some of it to increase their food-production capacity, and they buy food to eliminate the one- or two-month period of hunger most of them experienced each year before they increased their income. They also improve their year-round diets. Instead of a few morsels of meat or fish once a month if they are lucky, they regularly produce or buy meat and fish for their own consumption, augmented by milk from a goat or a buffalo and eggs from a few chickens. Most such families increase their income by growing fruits and vegetables, and they always eat the ones they can't sell, adding minerals and vitamins to their diet. Blindness in the children of poor families due to vitamin A deficiency disappears when the family starts consuming yellow or orange vegetables. Improved nutrition strengthens immune systems and lowers illness rates.

Water and Sanitation

In 1996 I lived in a village in Nepal for a week. Not one of the families in the village had a latrine. They did, however, have dogs, and when you did your business somewhere behind a bush, one of the dogs came along and ate it. Three of us had a cup of tea in a teahouse along a walking trail in the Nepal hills, and the undiapered two-year-old daughter of the woman who owned it pooped right next to our table. Undaunted, her mother immediately called over the dog, which dutifully consumed it. This sort of thing is more the norm than the exception in poor rural villages. The development community provides free latrines, which usually quickly reach a deplorable state because nobody cleans them. When IDE activated private-sector workshops in Vietnam to offer attractive, affordable latrines to rural customers and people started buying them at an unsubsidized price, the water and sanitation experts were amazed. That poor people might be willing to pay for their own latrines was a radical concept in the development field. A large number of dollar-a-day families are both willing and able, especially after they increase their income, to purchase hand pumps and latrines at a fair market price without subsidy.

Most poor people are now well informed about the advantages of having a source of clean household water, and are prepared to invest in it if it is available at an affordable price. But the world's water and sanitation experts have never put a high priority on making available hand pumps and clean-water systems that are cheap enough for poor families to afford, even when they increase their income. In Vietnam, when IDE was able to cut the market price of a serviceable UNICEF shallow-water hand pump in half and activated the private sector to deliver it, eighty thousand families installed affordable hand pumps, and since many were used by the neighbors, this opened access to clean drinking water to 2 million rural people.[59]

MULTIPLE-USE DRINKING WATER SYSTEMS[60]

Bahadur's family used one water source for both irrigation and household drinking water, a common behavior. Many families in Nepal's flat Tarai region use treadle pumps both to irrigate their vegetables and to provide clean drinking water for their homes. Sixty communities in hill areas of Nepal have now installed low-cost piped-water systems that carry water by gravity through pipes from clean springs and streams to provide both household water and water for drip-irrigated crops. The drip-irrigated cash crops generate enough income to pay for the system, and the modest fees paid by each household taking advantage of access to drinking water cover the operation and maintenance costs of the system, managed by a water-users' committee. This opens up the possibility that many new rural household water systems can become economically sustainable by taking advantage of the income generated by drip-irrigated cash crops or other productive ways the system's water is put to work.

Health

As soon as they realize that drinking bad water makes family members sick with diarrhea, with its potentially lethal effects on infants and the loss of work and income, poor families use their new income to invest in a clean water source for the household. They may already have invested in an affordable irrigation pump, and if it is located close enough to the house, they use it as a source of clean household water in addition to irrigation. If it doesn't cost too much, the family installs a well and a hand pump, and makes the water produced available to their neighbors. If an affordable water filter is available and a well isn't, the family buys a filter and uses it. If they have access to affordable latrines that fit their needs, they invest in a latrine. When a family member becomes ill, they can afford to go to a clinic and buy medicines, and they do so at a much earlier stage in the progression of the illness.

Education

When Bahadur's family increased their income, their education level soared. Bahadur's two wives remain illiterate, yet both his sons have finished high school and their wives have finished high school, and their children will stay in school as long as they like. Most of the rural children in countries like Nepal and Zambia stop going to school after grade five because their families can't afford the small amount of money required to buy books and school uniforms, and because they are needed at home to help with the farmwork. But if half the families in a village start to keep their children in school past grade five like Bahadur's grandchildren, tuition payments at the village school will increase, and perhaps they can attract a more qualified teacher—the teachers in many schools in poor villages are barely literate.

Transport

Many poor rural villages are served with roads that are barely passable, or no roads at all, constraining access to markets where small-acreage farmers can sell what they grow. Villagers can grow old waiting for the government to build a road. But there are other affordable transport options. The one poor people use most is their own two feet. Every small-plot farmer I have met is quite capable of balancing a wicker basket with twenty kilos of eggplant on his head and carrying it to a village market. I have interviewed porters in Nepal who, wearing nothing more than flip-flops on their feet, carry one hundred kilos on their back for six days over trails so steep they would qualify as mountain climbing in Western countries.

In Somalia, we helped refugee blacksmiths build five hundred donkey carts that operated well hauling half a ton of wood or water on rough dirt tracks. These carts, outfitted on used automotive bearings, were bought by refugees on credit for a price of four hundred fifty dollars US, and promptly started generating net income of two hundred dollars a month by hauling water, wood, and repackaged food. In Kathmandu, 7.5-hp Chinese diesel rototillers, imported without duty as agricultural equipment, pull trailers with one-ton loads of anything from people to coal up and down the hilly streets. In Vietnam I filmed bamboo frames hanging like painters' scaffolding from both sides of the frames of reinforced bicycles carrying up to four hundred kilos of bricks, with the owners walking alongside pushing the load forward by leaning into a stout bamboo pole attached to the seat post. These bamboo bicycle carriers helped win the Vietnam War by carrying supplies along the Ho Chi Minh trail, and have tremendous potential in rural areas because they can operate on single-file footpaths. But for some reason, I have never seen bamboo bicycle carriers used outside of Vietnam. In Bangladesh, I have seen trailers with wooden platforms pushed by two or three porters transporting large white bulls to be sacrificed for Eid. Apparently, the two or three kilos the bull might lose as a result of walking are more valuable than what it costs to pay three porters to push him along seated regally on a trailer. And then there are the motorcycles and the motorcycle trailers that carry vegetables and pigs and all kinds of cargo all over Cambodia. Even very poor people can afford the few pennies to hire a rickshaw in Bangladesh, and they use rickshaws to haul refrigerators and all kinds of lumpy goods that are too awkward or too big to carry on their backs.

People who survive on less than a dollar a day walk everywhere, occasionally hire a rickshaw for a lumpy load, and take the bus to cover longer distances when, for example, they travel to the city to look for work. When small-acreage farmers increase their income, many buy a used bicycle, and as income continues to rise, they invest in a bullock and a cart, and contract out on hauling jobs. A bullock cart or a bicycle trailer becomes a major source of income when used to transport high-value crops to markets or to haul inputs to the farm. Contract hauling in itself then can become an important source of income.

Housing

Governments and development organizations have launched many housing initiatives, but the subsidized housing is almost always far too expensive for dollar-a-day families, and if houses are given away, as they sometimes are, there is not enough money to build more than a tiny fraction of the homes that are needed. However, when poor people earn more income, they often invest in home improvements such as replacing a thatch roof with corrugated tin that doesn't leak. Others redo their dung and clay floors. Still others add a separate small kitchen to their courtyard, so their cooking fires don't overheat the main living space in summertime. Some build a more permanent house than the more common mud-and-wattle dwelling with a thatched roof. This house is likely to have real market and collateral value, but it may take ten or twelve years to build, twenty-five bricks at a time. As income from agriculture continues to increase, the house construction can speed up, and when the first module is completed, its collateral value can contribute to building a second and third module more quickly.

Energy

When Bahadur's family increased their income, they quickly bought two buffaloes, which now produce good income from milk. One of them is used to plow their one acre of rice down by the river, but they borrow seven more buffalo from neighbors, and the team of eight can plow an entire field in one day. Then the neighbors can use the Thapa family buffalo to help prepare their rice fields for planting. Bahadur's new house is now connected to electricity, but most of his neighbors can't afford it. The irrigation and drinking water they use flows gravity-fed through pipes from streams, and the closeness of a paved road with buses simplifies their transport needs. In all these respects, they are luckier than most small-acreage poor farmers.

After World War II, the US government–sponsored Rural Electrification Administration (REA) program made electricity widely available in the rural South, spurring economic development there. But more than 1 billion people in poor rural areas in developing countries will never be connected to the electric grid. Most of them are small-acreage farmers like Krishna Bahadur Thapa, who need energy every day to lift water, cultivate their fields, cook their meals, transport crops and inputs, carry out some value-added processing, and light their homes after dark. Human power is the main energy source, along with candles and kerosene and flashlight batteries to provide light, and wood for cooking. They spend three to five dollars a month on kerosene for their lamps, and on batteries and candles.

A range of new affordable technologies now available can enhance small-acreage farmers' use of energy and make it more efficient. For household lighting, solar lanterns with three times the light intensity of kerosene lamps are now available for a retail price of twelve dollars, with a payback period of less than six months from savings in kerosene, candles, and batteries, and as small-farm income increases, it soon will be possible to invest in a fifty-dollar solar home system that lights four rooms and powers a radio and a black-and-white television set.

Treadle pumps are a much more efficient way of using human power for irrigation than are buckets with a rope attached, and affordable drip-irrigation systems save energy used in water-lifting by reducing the amount of water needed to produce the same crop. Cook stoves that use less than half the firewood consumed by the three-stone method are now available for five dollars, and the poor have purchased hundreds of thousands of them. Low-cost household-level gasifiers, which are even more efficient and leave behind some salable charcoal after cooking a family meal, will soon be available.

Most small-plot farmers leave a much gentler footprint on the planet in their use of energy than do their large-farm neighbors. Human and animal power for water-lifting and cultivation burn renewable energy in the form of grain and fodder, compared with the diesel fuel consumed by the mechanized pumps and tractors used by their large-farm neighbors, and a farmer using his own legs to lift water is likely to be much more judicious in its use than is a neighbor turning on an electric pump by flicking a switch. A bullock cart runs on fodder, a form of renewable energy. A pickup truck burns gasoline.

Increasing small-farm income through growing cash crops makes its greatest contribution to the reduction of carbon emissions by shortening the transport chain from field to table. The rural poor routinely live with a food deficit that frequently turns into famine in times of drought or flood, requiring large amounts of food aid to be transported over great distances. As small farms increase their income by growing cash crops, they can afford to increase the yields of the subsistence crops they grow, and cover any deficits that remain by buying the food they need from their grain-growing large-farm neighbors. This more than makes up for the slight increase in transport energy used to bring their fruits and vegetables to market.

Ending poverty will not by itself address all the deficits poor people currently face in access to reasonable health, education, transport, water and sanitation, housing, and energy services. But it will make a remarkably significant contribution to solving each of these problems. By addressing the root cause of rapid population growth and helping find solutions to other root causes of poverty, helping millions of extremely poor people out of poverty will make a profound contribution to finding practical solutions to many of the key challenges facing the planet over the next fifty years. Nothing illustrates this better than the experience of Krishna Bahadur Thapa and his family.

Moving out of poverty in Zambia

CHAPTER ELEVEN

Taking Action to End Poverty

DEVELOPMENT DONORS, MULTINATIONAL CORPORATIONS, universities, agriculture and irrigation research institutions, ordinary people all over the world, and, most importantly, poor people themselves will need to adopt new ways of thinking about poverty and new ways of acting in order to end it.

What You Can Do

I wrote this book to create a revolution in how we think about poverty and what we do about it. That revolution begins with you.

I have been asked many times if the practical solutions to poverty in this book can also be applied to poverty in the United States. Of course they can! In one region of the Navajo Nation where the borders of Colorado, Arizona, and New Mexico meet, the Bureau of Indian Affairs (BIA) spends several million dollars every few years rehabilitating a canal that provides irrigation water to eight hundred poor rural

Navajo families. Many of these families live on welfare and use this precious water to grow grass for their riding ponies.

Yet I met a Navajo entrepreneur who works for the BIA and grows, processes, and packages steamed corn, and a variety of culturally valued corn products. He sells them to Navajo customers all over the United States. I met four or five other entrepreneurial Navajo farmers like him. Why couldn't these successful Navajo entrepreneurs serve as role models for hundreds of Navajos using low-cost drip irrigation and intensive horticulture to create and market a variety of branded culturally important high-value agricultural products? And why couldn't those of you interested in Native American culture help something like this come into being?

When I visited the San Luis Valley, the poorest rural area in Colorado, I learned that potatoes, one of the most economically important crops grown there, were trucked out of the San Luis Valley to Texas, where they were repackaged in five-pound bags, trucked back to San Luis Valley grocery stores, and sold at a decent markup. But the potato products with the greatest markups were frozen packaged french fries and curly fries, trucked back from Texas to San Luis Valley cafes and restaurants. Why not form local rural enterprises that process local potatoes into frozen french fries and curly fries and sell them to local restaurants? The savings in transport costs should more than make up for the "economies of scale" of bigger processing plants in Texas. Since a lot of canola is also grown in San Luis Valley, why not use low-cost oil expellers to produce a locally branded form of canola oil for local health food stores?

In the Introduction, I told the story of the things I learned from spending an afternoon with Joe, a homeless person who lived under a loading dock by the railroad yards in Denver. Most of you meet homeless people every day, and it's natural to turn your head away. But many homeless people have interesting stories to tell, and it's simple to ask the staff of the nearest homeless shelter to introduce you to one or two of them who are too quiet or shy to be panhandlers. Virtually all homeless people have a problem finding a safe place to store their stuff. What would it take to find an unused building in an area frequented by homeless people where some homeless people who are natural entrepreneurs could operate a safe storage-locker business serving other homeless people?

These are examples of the practical things you can do, if you live in the United States or Canada or Europe, to help solve the problem of poverty at home. But as you've probably guessed by now, the problem-solving process I describe in this book applies to many other important problems in the world beyond poverty. The practical solutions to many of the world's most difficult social problems lie in going to where the action is, listening to the people who have the problem, and learning everything there is to know about the problem's local context.

Practical Things You Can Do

1. If you like what you've read in this book, get ten other people to read it and encourage them to act on what they learn from it.

2. Stop pitying poor people.

3. Learn as much as you can about poor people in your neighborhood, their specific problems, and the specific context in which they live and work.

4. Become informed about the realities of global poverty and what can be done about it.

5. Invest in viable businesses serving poor customers.

6. Contribute time and money to organizations that demonstrate specific scalable impacts, and make them accountable for whatever time or money you provide.

What Poor People Can Do to End Their Own Poverty

1. Have hope.

2. Be willing to take some carefully calculated risks.

3. Don't depend too much on what the experts advise.

4. Be curious about new ideas and opportunities.

5. Be even more entrepreneurial than you are already.

6. Be generous in teaching development people what they need to know to become more effective.

What Donors Can Do to End Poverty

There are two major flaws in the way current donors deliver the funds they invest in poverty-eradication initiatives.

1. Some 80 percent of these funds flow directly through the governments of developing countries, and this simply hasn't worked.

2. Development donors don't insist that every investment produces measurable positive impacts and that these impacts can be scaled up to reach millions of people.

BILATERAL AND MULTILATERAL INVESTMENTS

Total official development assistance topped 100 billion dollars in 2005,[61] with 80 percent of it going directly to the governments of developing countries as bilateral or multilateral aid. According to the World Bank, 12 percent of development funding was delivered through nongovernmental organizations (NGOs) instead of governments.

Directing funding through the governments of developing countries is so much a part of the aid landscape that nobody seems to notice it anymore, much less question it. The thinking behind such a policy seems eminently reasonable. It's just as important for the government of a poor country to strengthen its own capacity to plan and to implement plans as it is to get critical roads and schools and hospitals built. Unfortunately, this approach simply has not worked, and some of the funding delivered through NGOs has also failed to produce positive measurable impacts.

The fact that major donors such as the United Nations Development Program (UNDP) can provide funding only through the governments of recipient countries sometimes creates unconscionable limitations. For example, the UN Millennium Development Goals initiative is blocked from funding projects in Myanmar because the government of Myanmar does not meet UN standards for good governance. This means that the rapidly growing numbers of extremely poor people in Myanmar's remote villages, who have little or no influence on who governs their country, are officially removed from United Nations assistance.

The solution to this dilemma is as difficult to implement as it is easy to visualize. Reverse the current ratio! Insist that 80 percent of current donor investments in development flows directly to the villages and urban slums where poor people earn their livelihoods and dream of a better future, and that 20 percent flows through the governments of developing countries.

WHY BILATERAL AND MULTILATERAL FUNDS ARE MISSPENT

By the time Joseph Mobutu left Zaire after thirty years of despotic rule, his net worth was equivalent to Zaire's national debt. But in spite of all the attention that corruption gets, it isn't the most important reason why so many projects that flow through the governments of poor countries fail to show results. The biggest reason is that the government leaders and their friends use their influence to direct the money to projects that may be of great interest to them but have no discernible impact on the major problems their countries face. Extremely poor people have little political influence, so it shouldn't be a big surprise that big development projects don't help them much.

Joseph Mobutu's government was able to obtain funding from multiple donors for a billion-dollar power line in Zaire, described by *Time* magazine as follows:

"Among Mobutu's development projects was a huge undertaking to dam the Zaire River and to build a 1,100-mile-long power line to the Shaba copper-producing region at a total estimated cost of about $1 billion. Eight months after the power was finally turned on in 1981, the current was switched off. Shaba province happens to be self-sufficient in electricity. Says one Western diplomat: "If ever there was a white elephant, this is it. Zaire needs the scheme as much as it needs a nuclear-powered submarine.""[62]

Mobutu and his friends undoubtedly reaped rich rewards by diverting funds from this project into their pockets, and could leave the responsibility for repayment of the loans involved to his successors, who will undoubtedly apply for one of the international rounds of debt forgiveness when the loans come due.

While Mobutu's power line may be an extreme example of the futility of directing funds through the governments of poor countries, the ultimate impact of many multilateral and bilateral projects is little better. In Nepal, for example, both the Chapakot Tar project, a favorite of the government's irrigation department, and the massive Arun III hydropower project were aborted after millions of dollars had already been spent, because the government leaders and their influential friends who supported these projects for self-serving reasons never realistically examined either the excessive cost of these projects or the more cost-effective and environmentally effective decentralized alternatives. In the same way in Africa, hundreds of millions of dollars of bilateral and multilateral funds have been spent on large and expensive irrigation systems backed by governments and their influential friends, without serious attempts to learn about much more affordable and cost-effective small irrigation systems that have great relevance both to ending the poverty of dollar-a-day rural families and to stimulating rural growth in most African countries.

For all of these reasons, it's time to reverse the ratio of where development funds are invested—we should invest 80 percent or more of development funds directly at the grassroots level, in initiatives with measurable impacts centered on increasing the income of very poor people, and invest the remaining 20 percent through the governments of developing countries in order to improve infrastructure. The funds that continue flowing to governments could be tied to specific deliverable outcomes, including public support of services in health, education, transport, energy, and the other key infrastructures that are so critical in sustaining poor families.

Since many of the 189 governments that have signed on to the Millennium Development Goals are those of developing countries, and these governments have powerful links to leaders in lending institutions and key development donors, such a ratio reversal is likely to be extremely difficult to accomplish. Such a sea change may require a new generation of lending and development institutions that are less tied to the governments of developing countries and their existing powerful sponsors. But to have any hope of implementing practical solutions to existing severe poverty, such a sea change is exactly what has to be accomplished.

TIE FUNDING TO MEASURABLE IMPACTS AND SCALABILITY

The Bill and Melinda Gates Foundation has two rules for funding a project, each of which is a very helpful condition.

1. No matter how promising any project sounds, if it can't define measurable impacts and attain them, the foundation won't invest in it.

2. If a project defines attainable impact, the Gates Foundation still won't invest in it unless it can be scaled up to reach large numbers of people.

If all development donors insisted on measurable impact and scalability for every penny of the $100 billion they invest every year in development initiatives, the results achieved by their poverty eradication initiatives would improve dramatically.

What Multinationals Can Do to End Poverty

Multinational corporations can make dramatic contributions to the end of poverty and, at the same time, to their own bottom-line profits, but that too will take a revolution in how they define, price, and deliver their products. In spite of the fact that Johnson and Johnson, a company in the international pharmaceuticals business, has presence and manufacturing capability in India, the company has not introduced Tylenol, a major profit-maker in developed markets, to India. Why not? Because it doesn't think it can make an attractive profit doing so. But implementing a price structure and a marketing-and-distribution strategy that compete in the Indian marketplace would be likely to produce attractive profits from higher volume even with lower-margin sales. It would also allow J and J to manufacture Tylenol at a lower price in India and export it to other countries.

Most pharmaceutical multinationals have a barely perceptible presence for both prescription and over-the-counter drugs in emerging markets. One US pharmaceutical leader said, "Latin America is not a place where you can ever make money."[63]

Contrast this with the statement made by Robert Wood "General" Johnson in 1943, as he set out to reform the pharmaceutical industry with the company that bore his name.

"Industry only has the right to succeed where it performs a real economic service and is a true social asset."[64]

If the pharmaceutical industry adopted General Johnson's 1943 credo, the lives of hundreds of millions of people in emerging markets, with illnesses ranging from HIV/AIDS to pneumonia, would improve. So would the bottom lines of international pharmaceutical companies.

This kind of institutionalized blindness is not limited to pharmaceutical companies. It prevents multinationals from providing a wide spectrum of products and services that 3 billion ignored customers desperately need and are eager to buy.

At a time of increasing water scarcity, drip irrigation, one of the most efficient ways of delivering water to plants, represents only 1 percent of global irrigated acreage. This is primarily because the drip-irrigation systems sold by existing companies are too big and too expensive for the small-farm mass market. At the same time, fully half of all the sales of the current global irrigation industry are made to golf courses. If only one in ten of the 485 million farms in the world less than five acres bought and installed half-acre low-cost drip systems designed to fit their small plots and wallets, global acreage under drip irrigation would triple. Yet both Netafim, the biggest drip-irrigation company in the world, and Jain Irrigation, the biggest drip-irrigation company in India, have politely but firmly rejected my repeated attempts to persuade their top leadership to enter the relatively untouched mass market for small, affordable drip systems.

In contrast, a small but increasingly influential group of multinationals is launching profitable initiatives that serve less affluent customers. Nestlé, the Swiss-based food giant, is recruiting small-plot coffee farmers to supply shade-grown specialty coffees to the millions of Europeans and North Americans who have bought its home espresso "Nesspresso" machines. Most of the 23 million small-plot coffee growers in the world don't have access to the coffee seedlings, the cutting-edge horticultural techniques, and the affordable irrigation required to grow these specialty coffees. So in Nicaragua, ECOM—the largest international coffee export company in the world, which provides much of the specialty coffee for Nestlé's "Nesspresso" machines—and Atlantic, an international coffee company that supplies Nestlé, are providing both new varieties of coffee seedlings and training programs for small-plot coffee growers. IDE's provision of access to affordable drip irrigation in side-by-side test plots has produced remarkable additional gains in yield and quality. If the scaling-up of this initial pilot program proves successful, ECOM/Nestlé and IDE plan a partnership applying this approach to small-plot coffee growers on a much larger scale in several developing countries, and to apply the same approach to small-farm tea and dairy production.

Thousands of opportunities like this exist for multinationals to make a direct positive impact on poverty eradication, and to improve their profits doing so.

What Universities Can Do

It should be no surprise that universities and research institutions have the same kinds of blind spots as multinational corporations. How can we expect professors of animal husbandry or agriculture or engineering at Colorado State University to teach graduate students from Nepal and Ethiopia and Malawi how to raise three goats profitably or how to cultivate a quarter acre of diversified off-season fruits and vegetables or to design a low-pressure half-acre sprinkler system that lasts three years? Yet teaching cutting-edge theory and practice in each of these topics will do more for poverty eradication in emerging markets than all the information currently being taught about animal husbandry factories or plantation monoculture, or the design of air-conditioned combines with more bells and whistles.

Ending poverty requires revolutionary changes in how we think and what we do about water, agriculture, markets, and design. There is no better place to start the revolution than universities like Wageningen, Stanford, Redding, CalTech, and MIT where so many of the professional and political leaders in developing countries go to get degrees. Since most of the world's dollar-a-day people earn their living from one-acre farms, entirely new courses and curricula need to be developed that focus on the farming, irrigation, market, and design needs of one-acre farms. Ending urban poverty requires radical new curricula teaching how to create new enterprises employing slum and pavement dwellers and new markets for high-value, labor-intensive products and services that take advantage of their low labor costs.

But the agendas of universities, and of the professors who teach in them, are shaped by the political and commercial contexts in which they operate. The land grant universities in the United States have a clear agriculture agenda, but it is an agenda that focuses on continuing to improve the efficiency of the large, mechanized farms and large livestock operations that make up agriculture in developed countries. Many of the professors who teach agriculture, business, irrigation, and design earned their PhDs working on topics dealing with big-farm and big-machinery problems, and these are the same areas in which the grants that are a university's lifeblood are concentrated. So professors teach what they know, and bright young students from developing countries get useful training in Western agriculture and design that has little or no relevance in their own countries.

The good news is that the students themselves are asking their professors to help them learn how to change all this. Jim Patell, a professor at Stanford School of Business who is a principal architect of Stanford Design School's course "Design for Extreme Affordability," tells me that ten years ago, the typical student who came to Stanford to get an MBA said, "Teach me to be Bill Gates."

Now he or she is more likely to say, "Teach me to make a difference."

Of course, now Bill Gates has handed over the leadership of Microsoft and is devoting most of his life to making a difference too.

A major concern, of course, is that if universities are successful in helping students learn to make a difference in the world, how will these graduates make a living at it? A few brave souls are already starting their own companies and development organizations, and a few more go to work for organizations such as Mercy Corps or Helvetas or Winrock or SKAT or IDE. But the real job opportunities will come from the commercial sector as multinationals and a range of large and small enterprises increasingly create new ventures that serve the other 90 percent of customers who aren't now being served.

What Research Institutions Can Do

Many of the people who teach in universities also consult or work for research institutions working on development problems. The Consultative Group on International Agricultural Research (CGIAR), which carries out research to support the green revolution, has been remarkably effective in increasing the world's food supply. Lowering the real price of food helps poor people. But ending poverty requires the creation of research institutions generating new thinking and new practice for increasing the incomes of poor people in rural and urban areas.

The Small-Farm Prosperity Network

I propose we form a network of centers, comparable in size and scope to the CGIAR network, called the Small-Farm Prosperity Network, with an annual budget in the range of $350 million, focused on research and innovative practice to create new income on the one-acre farms where some 800 million dollar-a-day people now earn their livings. The centers in this network would include:

THE AFFORDABLE SMALL-FARM IRRIGATION CENTER

A revolution in irrigation is needed to design and disseminate a range of new low-cost irrigation technologies that fit the needs of one-acre farms. The International Water Management Institute (IWMI), a part of the current CGIAR system, has in the past few years begun to do important work in this field, but its main emphasis remains research on large irrigation systems and ways to manage them more effectively. IDE recently received support from the Gates Foundation to bring thirteen different small-plot irrigation technologies to the market-ready point, including a variety of affordable small-farm water-lifting, water-storage, and water-distribution technologies. But IDE is a comparatively small organization, and while other organizations such as KickStart and EnterpriseWorks/Vita have made important contributions, especially in the design and private-sector distribution of treadle pumps, the whole field would benefit from the creation of a research and dissemination center focusing on the development and mass dissemination of affordable small-farm irrigation tools.

THE CENTER FOR INNOVATION IN MULTIPLE-USE SYSTEMS

I have previously pointed out the opportunities that exist for integrating the creation of village drinking-water systems with the income opportunities that can be derived from concurrently using the water made available by new drinking-water systems to irrigate intensively cultivated small-horticulture crops. IDE, IWMI, and several other organizations have already demonstrated that the income from productive use of some of the water originating from multiple-use systems is sufficient to pay off a loan for the construction of the system. A center charged with facilitating the rapid dissemination of multiple-use systems and carrying out research in the field would open economically sustainable access to new sources of household water for millions of people who don't have it now, and would provide new sources of irrigation water capable of increasing the incomes of millions of small-plot farmers.

THE SMALL-FARM PROSPERITY AGRICULTURE CENTER

Ending poverty requires a revolution in agriculture focusing on income-generating crops for small farms. The Small-Farm Prosperity Agriculture Center will develop new varieties of labor-intensive, marketable cash crops for one-acre farms, the cultivation methods required to grow them, and the business practices required to sell them at an attractive profit.

THE CENTER FOR CREATING NEW PROSPERITY FOR THE LANDLESS

Virtually all "landless" people in the rural areas of developing countries are not functionally landless. Most of them have access to one hundred to five hundred square meters of land provided by their landlords or by village commons areas. In IDE Nepal, small-plot farmers are earning net incomes of as much as two hundred dollars by growing monsoon-season tomatoes, and most landless families already expand their crop area by growing squash vines on their rooftops and planting one or two papaya trees for their family's use. The Center for Creating New

Prosperity for the Landless will conduct competitions for generating the greatest income on one hundred square meters, develop intensive horticultural techniques for optimizing income from small plots of land, and research ways for landless people to increase their incomes.

THE CENTER FOR CREATING NEW MARKETS THAT SERVE POOR CUSTOMERS

A revolution in markets is to understand and find ways to address the glaring inefficiencies of the existing markets where dollar-a-day urban and rural people are buyers and sellers. The Center for Creating New Markets That Serve Poor Customers will identify Henry Ford–size opportunities in the rural and urban markets, and take practical action to exploit them. In rural areas, the center will facilitate the emergence of private-sector supply chains providing small-acreage farmers with the irrigation, seeds, fertilizer, pest management, and credit they need to grow high-value, labor-intensive crops, and the value chains that help them gain access to markets where they can sell their crops at a profit. In urban areas, the center will facilitate the emergence of new job-creating enterprises and new markets for high-value, labor-intensive products that can harness the low-cost labor of slum and pavement dwellers.

What Development Organizations Can Do

From grassroots village organizations in India, with budgets of a few hundred dollars, to giant international organizations such as World Vision, with an annual budget of $1.1 billion, there are thousands of development organizations in the world working on poverty issues. Their main shortcoming is that few of them know anything much about how to make money, and they have little or no motivation to learn how to do so. The problem with this is that helping poor people to make more money is the single most important thing anyone can do to end poverty.

When I started IDE in 1981, business was a dirty word to the development community, which regarded the profiteering of multinationals and other commercial firms as a root cause of poverty. Over the last fifteen years, there has been a growing realization by development workers that not all businesses are evil and that effective business strategies provide important tools for poverty alleviation. In spite of this, most development organizations give things away, operate in ways that undercut sustainable market forces, and build their missions and their fund-raising strategies around the good feeling you get when you donate something of value to a poor person who needs it.

The poverty of millions of dollar-a-day people would end if development organizations adopted a few basic principles:

1. Talk to as many poor people as you can before you start any programs, and learn as much as you can about the specific contexts where they live and work.

2. If you have a product or a service that you think is valuable for poor people, design it to sell at a price that is affordable at their present income level. If they don't elect to buy it, change it or drop it.

3. Treat poor people as customers for goods and services instead of as recipients of charity.

4. Stop giving things away, and oppose government and donor subsidies.

5. Design and distribute income-generating products and services for dollar-a-day people that provide a net return of 300 percent a year or more on their investments.

6. Promote the emergence of profitable private-sector supply chains to sell poor people the things they need at a fair market price, and profitable private-sector value chains that allow them to sell what they produce at an attractive profit.

7. Open access to credit.

I fully realize that a public investment is needed in areas such as health, education, and transport, the same as there is in countries with mature markets. But in many developing countries, the money simply isn't there for the government to provide the roads and health care and education that poor people need. But when they gain access to new sources of income, poor people continue to astonish me with what they are able to do for themselves.

What Designers Can Do: Design for the Other 90 Percent

If all the creative problem-solvers in the field of design address only the problems of the richest 10 percent of the world's customers, a revolution in design is needed to incorporate the needs of the other 90 percent. This requires radical changes in the way design is taught both in rich and in developing countries, and building a platform so that at least ten thousand of the world's best designers focus their attention on products and services that meet the needs of the other 90 percent of the world's population.

One hundred graduate engineering, business, and humanities students apply each year to get into the course "Design for Extreme Affordability" run by Jim Patell and David Kelly at the Stanford Design School, and forty get in. This course incorporates the principles of design based on the ruthless pursuit of affordability that I have outlined, and the students work in multidisciplinary design teams on practical village problems they have selected after IDE-facilitated trips to villages in countries such as Myanmar. The output on which each team is graded includes not only the quality and affordability of the design of a cutting-edge income-generating technology they have prototyped and field-tested, but also on an elevator pitch, a short video, and a realistic business plan. In 2007 one team designed an improved and more affordable treadle pump for Myanmar, took it to Myanmar in the summer after the course ended, introduced it to the marketplace, and received orders from poor farmers for two thousand within two weeks after its introduction to the market.

For many years, Amy Smith has been taking undergraduate students at MIT working on village designs to countries such as Haiti, Zambia, India, and Ghana, and students at Cal Tech recruited Ken Pickar, a gifted space engineer, to teach a course addressing design problems for Guatemala. To improve communication with village environments, this course linked up with a university in Guatemala, and design teams now include a student from Guatemala working on each problem.

The design revolution will harness the energy of ten thousand of the world's best designers. I had a lunch meeting with some of them on the occasion of the launch of the Smithsonian Cooper-Hewitt National Design Museum exhibit "Design for the Other 90 Percent," inspired by my ideas. Bart Voorsanger, of Voorsanger Architects PC in New York which designs large private dwellings and public buildings, was fascinated by the challenge of designing a hundred-dollar house, and I will meet with his firm during 2007 to discuss how it might participate.

A few years ago, I believed that professors teaching irrigation in universities simply showed a callous disregard for addressing village irrigation problems. Then Jack Keller, a retired professor of civil engineering at Utah State who is a world expert on irrigation, invited me to participate in a brainstorming discussion with irrigation academics at their annual meeting. They were fascinated by the possibility of applying what they knew about one-hundred-sixty-acre center-pivot sprinkler systems to designing a low-pressure, low-cost, half-acre sprinkler system for a small farm, and they were ready to help.

Enter the new organization I started in 2007, called D-Rev: Design for the Other Ninety Percent. (D-Rev, of course, stands for Design Revolution.) The mission of this new organization is to make the design revolution a reality.

One of its first projects is to work with the Gates Foundation to design a 1-hp diesel engine that will do for small-acreage farmers what the Toyota Prius did for cars. It will be designed to run with optimal efficiency and low emissions on biofuels grown and processed locally. On the drawing board is an international company to distribute 500 million two-dollar reading glasses, the hundred-dollar house, and a solar-powered water-purifying technology capable of delivering one thousand gallons of marketable drinking water a day at an investment cost for an entrepreneur of less than one hundred dollars.

I have no illusions that D-Rev will create the design revolution all by itself. My dream remains the same as when I started IDE: to create an effective working model that will energize the design revolution and spread it quickly around the world.

Twelve members of the Thapa family, 2007

CHAPTER TWELVE

Bahadur and His Family Move Out of Poverty

KRISHNA BAHADUR THAPA'S FAMILY'S ASSETS CONTINUED TO grow. Once he and his family had enough money to buy fertilizer and better seeds, they switched to more productive green revolution rice seeds, and the yield from their acre of rice by the river went up from twelve hundred fifty kilos each year to twenty-two hundred fifty kilos. But now his sons, Deu Bahadur Thapa and Puspa, were married and had children, so there were ten mouths to feed instead of six, and the family came out at the end of the year at about the same place they were before. They grew enough rice to feed themselves, and earned fifty to one hundred dollars in a good year from rice sales.

On the next page are the field notes about the Thapa family's rice production, exactly as I received them from the Nepali agronomist who works for IDE and lives half an hour from Ekle Phant.

Bahadur's family invested some of their new income in livestock, and earned considerable income from selling milk and goats for meat. It seemed that Krishna Bahadur Thapa and his family were leaving behind the poverty that they had always known. Then tragedy struck.

FIELD NOTES ON KRISHNA BAHADUR THAPA

Paddy Production

a. **Now**

Variety:	Mansuli
Production:	2,250 Kg (45 Muri); 1 Muri = 50 Kg
Fertilizer:	Urea– 8 Kg, DAP– 5 Kg, Potassium– 2 Kg, for surface dressing additional 15 Kg urea is used. Organic manure– 300 Doko (10,500 Kg); 1 Doko = 35 Kg After husking they have approximately 1,350 Kg of rice.

b. **Past**

Variety:	Local
Production:	1,250 Kg (25 Muri) (Production is sufficient for family. Sometimes they sold remaining rice because they had fewer members in family.)
Fertilizer:	Organic manure

The Death of Krishna Bahadur Thapa

On February 16, 2005, Krishna Bahadur Thapa was having a normal day. Although his doctor had diagnosed high blood pressure and Bahadur was taking medicine for it, he continued to feel fine. On that evening, the family enjoyed a good supper of goat meat, rice, dahl, and vegetables. Bahadur particularly enjoyed a pudding made from the blood of the goat they had slaughtered. After supper, Bahadur had a drink or two of *raksi*, a traditional alcohol distilled from millet that the family made with a still in their courtyard. He went to bed early. He was found dead at four the next morning. The doctor diagnosed a heart attack as the cause of death.

On January 25, 2007, I went to see Bahadur's son and his family to learn as much as I could about how and why Bahadur had died, and to find out how the family was doing. The head of the family was now

Krishna Bahadur Thapa's new house

Bahadur's older son, Deu Bahadur Thapa, age thirty. He welcomed me warmly to his home when I arrived just before noon. I found out only at the end of the day that he had missed an important meeting of the orange growers' co-op to spend the day with me.

I worried that Bahadur Thapa's new prosperity may have contributed to his death. Had his diet, now richer in meat, increased his blood levels of bad cholesterol or increased his consumption of raksi? But his son Deu told me that few people live to their sixties in Nepal, and Bahadur had died a happy man at the age of sixty-three. He said that although Bahadur drank some raksi from time to time, he had not become a heavy drinker. Knowing how hard he and his family had struggled because they were poor, I have no doubt that Bahadur experienced some of the happiest years of his life when he knew that he and his family had left poverty behind forever.

Deu Bahadur Thapa now gave me some exciting news. By the time I visited in January 2007, two years after Bahadur's death, his family was earning an astounding $4,816 US per year from a variety of enterprises. After expenses, they were left with $4,008 a year in net income, about

Krishna Bahadur Thapa's family has four oxen, one cow, four goats, and four buffaloes, and sells ten liters of milk a day.

twenty times as much as five years earlier, and much more than the income earned by most IDE Nepal staff members.

The Thapa family now irrigates a full acre (four thousand square meters) of vegetables, and last year vegetable sales brought in a total of $2,185. Vegetables are the family's biggest single source of income. Out of the thirteen vegetable varieties they grow, off-season cucumber and cauliflower generate the most income—$542 from cucumbers and $417 from cauliflower—with another $222 earned from tomatoes.

Current Irrigation Practice

Of the total of one acre (four thousand square meters) of irrigated vegetables, one thousand square meters are irrigated by drip, twenty-five hundred square meters by sprinkler, and five hundred square meters of very hilly land is irrigated by hand with a hose. Since a new village drinking-water system was installed by the Youth Foundation, the original Helvetas system is used only for irrigation, and sixteen families are now using it instead of the eight families using it five years ago.

Deu Bahadur now has a second half-inch irrigation pipe from another stream that also provides water twenty-four hours a day, seven days a week. He told me that out of the total of seventy-two families in Ekle Phant, sixty-six are now growing irrigated off-season vegetables, three times the number when I visited five years earlier. As I walked with Deu up to some of the new water sources, I saw that the whole landscape was festooned with black half-inch hoses winding their way over tree branches to irrigated vegetable plots.

Bringing the Family's Vegetables to Market

Instead of having to decide every day whether to sell their vegetables from a stall in the market, to hawkers, or to wholesalers, the family now sells all its vegetables at much better prices through the village

Vegetable	Land covered (ropani) (500 sq. m.)	Land covered (hectares) (10,000 sq. m.)	Production (Kg)	Sales (Rupees)	Sales ($)
Cauliflower	5	0.25	1,500	30,000	416.67
Cabbage	1	0.05	500	5,000	69.44
Cucumber	5	0.25	2,600	39,000	541.67
Potato	3	0.15	800	9,600	133.33
Chili	1	0.05	50	1,000	13.89
Tomato	2	0.10	800	16,000	222.22
Betel Gourd (Karela)	1	0.05	500	10,000	138.89
Gourd (Ghiraula)	5	0.25	1,200	11,250	156.25
Beans	6	0.30	900	18,000	250.00
Eggplant	1	0.05	500	5,000	69.44
Pumpkin	1	0.05	200	2,000	27.78
Radish	1	0.05	300	1,500	20.83
Green Vegetables			Lump Sum	5,000	69.44
Others			Lump Sum	4,000	55.55
Total				**157,350**	**2,185.40**

Table 10: Vegetable Production and Income for Deu Bahadur and His Family, 2006

Beans from the Thapa farm on the way to the Ekle Phant collection center

marketing center. In the past three years, IDE and its partner Winrock International have worked with many grassroots organizations to organize more than sixty village collection centers, each of which rents a small warehouse called a *godown* and hires a commissioned sales agent with a cell phone. One family might produce eight kilos a day of

Details	Income/Annum (Rupees)	Income ($)
Service (from Qatar)	95,000	1,319.44
Fishery	3,500	48.61
Orange sell	25,000	347.22
Goat sell	15,000	208.33
Milk sell	50,000	694.44
Others (from millet, etc.)	1,000	13.88
Total	189,500	2,631.94

Table 11: Other Income

eggplant, but seventy families produce enough to attract traders, and the sales agents provide rapid feedback about market demand and quality preferences that farmers can incorporate into their growing and grading practices. A farmers' marketing committee runs the Ekle Phant collection center—named Pragati Taja Flafhul Thatha Tarakari Samuhan, meaning "Pragati Fresh Fruits and Vegetables Group." The commission agent who works for the committee sells to a variety of buyers at Damauli, Mugling, and Dhumre.

A Cornucopia of Grassroots Enterprises

In addition to their vegetable business, the Thapa family has diversified. Tables 11 and 12 summarize the income from the family's other enterprises, and their yearly expenses, exactly as they were reported to me.

The Thapa family had blossomed to ten members. Puspa Bahadur Thapa, Krishna Bahadur Thapa's younger son, now age twenty-six, had been married in 2005. Where before, the family had struggled to earn a hundred dollars a year, now they had spent five hundred fifty-five dollars on the wedding celebrations. Puspa had a two-month-old daughter. Her grandmother rocked her gently in a swing made out of a long piece of blue cloth while I talked to Deu Bahadur Thapa.

I learned that the family had made a major investment in livestock. They now own four oxen, one cow, four buffaloes (including two calves), and four goats. They bought one adult milking buffalo for

Details	Amount (Rupees)	Amount ($)
Food & Clothing	40,000	555.55
Education	10,000	138.89
Medical	12,000	166.67
Festival	15,000	208.33
Total	**77,000**	**1,069.44**

Table 12: Expenditure

The family raises fish fingerlings to sell to fish farmers for their ponds.

twenty thousand rupees, and raised the other three from calves. They sell an average of ten liters a day of milk from two buffaloes.

They also keep three traditional beehives, short pieces of hollowed-out logs hung by wires from support beams outside their house. They don't sell honey—they consume all they produce.

Two years ago, the family paid 25,000 rupees for five ropanis of land (about two-thirds of an acre) with orange trees a two-hour walk from their home in the hills above it, and immediately began to plant more oranges. In 2006 they earned $347 from the orange grove. They earned an additional $208 by selling goats for meat, and $694 by selling buffalo milk. From a friend in the government's fisheries department, Krishna Bahadur Thapa learned that there was a shortage of fingerlings for fishponds, so he dug a small pond and started raising tilapia fingerlings from spawn he got from the fisheries department. The family earned only $49 from raising fingerlings last year, but hopes to expand their minnow venture next year.

Finally, two years ago, Krishna Bahadur Thapa's younger son, Puspa Bahadur Thapa, immigrated to Qatar on an eighteen-month contract with an oil company. I learned that getting a good labor contract like this was not easy. The family had to pay 70,000 rupees in cash up front to a labor contractor to get the job, and labor contractors often cheat their clients. The family paid part of the amount in cash and got a loan for the rest, and Puspa was able to pay everything back within nine months. After covering his expenses, he sent home $1,319 in 2006. During the Maoist uprising, many families in Nepal sent their sons overseas to get them out of harm's way. Many rural families in Nepal receive remittances from family members overseas—in earlier days, these were from Gurkha soldiers serving in the British army, and nowadays they are from contract jobs in the Middle East.

How the Thapa Family Invests Its New Income

As soon as Krishna Bahadur Thapa and his family started to earn new income, they invested part of it in education. While both of Bahadur's wives are illiterate, both his sons completed high school, Puspa's wife completed grade seven, and Deu Bahadur's wife completed grade eight. All of Krishna's grandchildren will continue to go to school as long as they can and want to. In 2006 the family invested $139 in education. Table 13 shows the family's current educational status.

Of course, the family's diet has improved enormously. In 2006 they spent $556 on food and clothing. They eat vegetables with every meal, which provides vitamins, minerals, and diversity, and from relying almost solely on rice and lentils as their protein source, they now add portions of fish and meat.

Two years ago, the family built a brand-new, two-story house of cement and stone, at a cost of $2,083. In my astonishment, I bumped my head when I went upstairs to see and film the new cement rice-storage bin. Unfortunately, because the bin had no sealed lid, rats were consuming 10 percent of the rice stored there.

The family can now afford to get health care quickly if somebody falls sick. Perhaps, after all, Krishna Bahadur Thapa's life had been prolonged by the blood pressure medication he was taking. They spent $167 on medical services in 2006.

I know all this sounds a little bit too good to be true, and one

Name	Age	Education	Relation
Mrs. Padam Maya Magar	56	Illiterate	1st wife of K. B. Thapa
Mrs. Sumitra Maya Magar	48	Illiterate	2nd wife of K. B. Thapa
Mr. Deu Bahadur Thapa	30	SLC pass	Elder son
Mrs. Devi Maya Magar	31	8th class pass	Wife of Mr. Deu Bahadur
Mr. Puspa Bahadur Thapa	26	SLC pass	Younger son
Mrs. Kali Thapa Magar	24	7th class pass	Wife of Mr. Puspa
Master Lok Bahadur Thapa	8	3 class running	Son of Mr. Deu Bahadur
Miss Saraswati Maya Magar	12	4 class running	Daughter of Mr. Deu Bahadur
Miss Ohm Maya Magar	10	4 class running	Daughter of Mr. Deu Bahadur
Miss Tara Maya Magar	2 months	Infant	Daughter of Mr. Puspa

Table 13: Thapa Family Information, September 2006

might suspect that I chose to tell the story of an exceptionally success-ful family after the fact. But I didn't do that. I picked Krishna Bahadur Thapa and his family to write about when I visited him five years ago, at a time when he was growing just a quarter acre of vegetables and earning five hundred dollars a year in new income. I decided to tell his story then, because he struck me as an entrepreneur and an innovator, and I had a good feeling about him and his family. I was shocked by the news of his death, and didn't know about how prosperous his fam-ily had become until I visited them in early 2007.

Of course, most dollar-a-day farmers don't do as well as have Baha-dur and his family. But most of them can increase their net annual income by at least five hundred dollars by growing a quarter acre of in-tensely cultivated off-season fruits and vegetables. And virtually all of the farmers I have interviewed invest part of their newly earned wealth in improved education for their children, improved diet, improved housing, and most of all, in continuing to improve the income they earn from farming.

There are 800 million dollar-a-day rural families like Krishna Bahadur Thapa's. Two hundred million or so of these families are officially classified as landless but have functional access to enough land to earn fifty to one hundred dollars a year in new net income by growing high-value cash crops. Six hundred million of them have access to at least a quarter acre of land, enough to increase their net annual income by five hundred dollars or more, just as Krishna Bahadur's family did. Another 300 million or more dollar-a-day people live in urban slums or on sidewalks. Like their rural brothers, they have great opportunities to increase their income by taking advantage of their low-cost labor to produce high-value, labor-intensive products and deliver them through new market mechanisms to more prosperous customers.

Of course, many people tell me that if so many poor farmers grow off-season fruits and vegetables, they will quickly flood the market. I heard this prediction for twenty years in Bangladesh, and even after we sold 1.5 million treadle pumps and put seven hundred fifty thousand acres under irrigation, the market wasn't flooded, other than the normal fluctuations experienced in every market. Demand for crops and vegetables expands rapidly in most developing countries as incomes increase, and the fact is that small-acreage farmers don't have to corner the market to thrive—they just have to be able to have a comparative advantage with larger-acreage farmers that enables small-plot farmers to sell even when large farms compete with them.

I have known several dollar-a-day families that are just as successful as Krishna Bahadur Thapa. One family I met in Himachal Pradesh, two-and-a-half hours by road and another three-and-a-half hours by train from Delhi, started growing a variety of flowers for the Delhi market. Fascinated by what they were doing, I left my card. I got an e-mail three years later, sent from the family's computer, asking how I was doing. The business had grown rapidly. Flowers were delivered to the railroad by truck in the middle of the night when refrigeration wasn't required, and sold in the Delhi flower market at five a.m.

But even if Krishna Bahadur and his family are the only family that moved in the space of several years from barely having enough to eat to earning four thousand dollars a year and rapidly becoming even more prosperous, why isn't the example of one family enough to bring hope to the others? If Krishna Bahadur's family can move out of poverty, educate their children, and improve their diet, health, and housing along the way, then, given the opportunity, many of the 1.2 billion dollar-a-day people in the world can do the same thing.

NOTES

CHAPTER 1

1. http://thinkprogress.org/2005/09/01/fema-director-we-did-not-know-new-orleans-convention-center-was-a-hurricane-shelter.

CHAPTER 2

2. William Easterly, "Was Development Assistance a Mistake?" *The American Economic Review* Vol. 97, No. 2 (May 2007).

3. William Easterly, *The White Man's Burden: Why the West's Efforts to Aid the Rest Have Done So Much Ill and So Little Good* (New York: Penguin Press, 2006).

4. Easterly, "Was Development Assistance a Mistake?"

5. Easterly, "Was Development Assistance a Mistake?"

6. http://news.bbc.co.uk/2/hi/science/nature/3397393.stm.

7. United Nations Department of Economic and Social Affairs (UNDESA), Millennium Development Goals Report 2006. http://mdgs.un.org/unsd/mdg/Resources/Static/Products/Progress2006/MDGReport2006.pdf.

8. UNDESA, Millennium Development Goals Report 2006.

9. The figures in this table have been corrected for inflation.

10. UNDESA, Millennium Development Goals Report 2006.

11. UNDESA, Millennium Development Goals Report 2006.

12. Food and Agriculture Organization of the United Nations, The State of Food Insecurity in the World 2004, p. 8. www.fao.org/docrep/007/y5650e/y5650e00.htm.

13. UNDESA, Millennium Development Goals Report 2006.

14. UNDESA, Millennium Development Goals Report 2006.

15. UNDESA, Millennium Development Goals Report 2006.

16. C.K. Prahalad, *The Fortune at the Bottom of the Pyramid* (Upper Saddle River, N.J.: Wharton School Publishing, 2005).

17. Prahalad, *The Fortune at the Bottom of the Pyramid*.

CHAPTER 3

18. Paul Hunt, Manfred Nowak, and Siddiq Osmani, *Human Rights and Poverty Reduction: A Conceptual Framework* (New York and Geneva: UN, 2004), p. 16.

CHAPTER 4

19. Cooper-Hewitt Exhibit Catalog, *Design for the Other 90%* (New York: Cooper-Hewitt National Design Museum, 2007).

20. Media coverage has included *The New York Times, Wall Street Journal, International Herald Tribune,* and Wisconsin National Public Radio stations.

21. Incorporated in Colorado in 2007, D-Rev is in the process of launching three international businesses serving poor customers while it supports the design revolution described in this book.

CHAPTER 5

22. Hunger Report 2005, "A Conversation with Dr. Norman Borlaug on the Past, Present, and Future of Hunger in the Developing World," Fifteenth Annual Report on the State of World Hunger, p. 27. http://www.bread.org/learn/hunger-reports/hunger-report-pdfs/hunger-report-2005/Chapter-1.pdf.

CHAPTER 6

23. Paul Polak, "The Design Process for the IDE Low-Cost Drip-Irrigation System," in "Poverty Alleviation as a Business. The Market Creation Approach to Development," by Urs Heierli and Paul Polak, Swiss Agency for Development and Cooperation (May 2000), pp. 95–100.

24. Sandra Postel, Paul Polak, Fernando Gonzales, and Jack Keller, "Drip Irrigation for Small Farmers: A New Initiative to Alleviate Hunger and Poverty," *Water International* Vol. 26, No. 1 (March 2001), pp. 3–13.

25. G.A. Cornish and P. Lawrence, *Informal Irrigation in Periurban Areas: A Summary of Findings and Recommendations* (United Kingdom: H.R. Wallingford, 2001).

26. Rob Gallagher, *The Rickshaws of Bangladesh* (Dhaka University Press, 1992).

CHAPTER 7

27. Oksana Nagayets, "Small Farms: Current Status and Key Trends," Future of Small Farms Research Workshop (held by International Food Policy Research Institute/2020 Vision Initiative, the Overseas Development Institute, and Imperial College, London), Wye College, United Kingdom, June 26–29, 2005. Washington, D.C.: International Food Policy Research Institute (IFPRI). Tables 1–4 in The Future of Small Farms reproduced with permission from the International Food Policy Research Institute, www.ifpri.org. The workshop proceedings from which these tables come can be found online at www.ifpri.org/events/seminars/2005/smallfarms/sfproc/sfproc.pdf.

28. Nagayets, Table 1, "Small Farms: Current Status and Key Trends." Reproduced with permission of IFPRI.

29. Nagayets, Table 2, "Small Farms: Current Status and Key Trends." Reproduced with permission of IFPRI.

30. Nagayets, Table 3, "Small Farms: Current Status and Key Trends." Reproduced with permission of IFPRI.

31. Nagayets, Table 3, "Small Farms: Current Status and Key Trends." Reproduced with permission of IFPRI.

32. Nagayets, Table 4, "Small Farms: Current Status and Key Trends." Reproduced with permission of IFPRI.

33. Nagayets, "Small Farms: Current Status and Key Trends." Reproduced with permission of IFPRI.

34. Regassa, E. Namara, Parakrama Weligamage, and Randolph Barker, *Prospects for Adopting System of Rice Intensification in Sri Lanka: A Socioeconomic Assessment* (Colombo, Sri Lanka: International Water Management Institute, 2002). http://www.iwmi.cgiar.org/pubs/pub075/Report75.pdf.

35. Norman Uphoff, "The System of Rice Intensification: Using Alternative Cultural Practices to Increase Rice Production and Profitability from Existing Yield Potentials," International Rice Commission Newsletter, No. 55, Food and Agriculture Organization (Rome: 2007).

36. http://www.iwmi.cgiar.org/livelihoods/index.htm.

37. The Future of Small Farms: Proceedings of a Research Workshop, Wye College, United Kingdom, June 26–29, 2005. Washington, D.C.: IFPRI.

38. J.R. Burleigh, L.L. Black, Lun G. Mateo, et al., "Performance of Grafted Tomato in Central Luzon, Philippines: A Case Study of the Introduction of a New Technology Among Resource-limited Farmers," Plant Management Network, July 1, 2005. http://www.plantmanagementnetwork.org/pub/cm/management/2005/tomato.

CHAPTER 8

39. The Energy Foundation, Bellagio Memorandum on Motor Vehicle Policy (Bellagio, Italy: 2001).

40. Paul Polak, "How IDE Installed 1.3 Million Treadle Pumps in Bangladesh by Activating the Private Sector," in "Poverty Alleviation as a Business. The Market Creation Approach to Development," by Urs Heierli and Paul Polak, Swiss Agency for Development and Cooperation (May 2000), pp. 101–108.

41. www.technoserve.org/africa/ghana-pineapple.html.

42. www.technoserve.org/africa/ghana-pineapple.html.

43. www.adaptive-eyecare.com/technology.html.

44. www.neweyesfortheneedy.org/vision/faqs.html.

45. Graham Macmillan, personal communication, January 2007.

CHAPTER 9

46. Kalpana Sharma, *Rediscovering Dharavi: Stories from Asia's Largest Slum* (India: Penguin Books India, 2000), pp. 75–78.

47. http://www.communityplanning.net/makingplanningwork/mpwcasestudies/mpwCS05.htm.

48. Pietro Garau, Elliot Sclar, and Gabriella Carolini, *A Home in the City: Improving the Lives of Slum Dwellers* (London: Earthscan, 2005), p. 11.

49. Sharma, *Rediscovering Dharavi: Stories from Asia's Largest Slum*, pp. 75–78.

50. UN-HABITAT Publication. http://www.un.org/Pubs/chronicle/2006/issue2/0206p24.htm.

51. UN-HABITAT Publication. http://www.un.org/Pubs/chronicle/2003/issue4/0403p19.asp.

52. United Nations Settlement Program, *The Challenge of Slums. Global Report on Human Settlements 2003* (New York: UN Publications, 2003), pp. 103–104. http://www.unhabitat.org/pmss/getPage.asp?page=bookView&book=1156.

53. Garau, Sclar, and Carolini, *A Home in the City.*

54. http://news.bbc.co.uk/1/shared/spl/hi/world/06/dharavi_slum/html/dharavi_slum_5.stm.

55. Steve Haggblade, J. Boomgard, S. Davies, and D. Mead, "Subsector Analysis: Its Nature, Conduct, and Potential Distribution to Small Enterprise Development," Department of Economics, Michigan State University. http://ideas.repec.org/p/msu/idpwrk/026.html.

56. Marina Samuf, "Favela fashion brings pride and jobs to Brazilian slum," *Brazzil Magazine* (August 2, 2006). http://www.brazzil.com/index.php?option=com_content&task=video&id=9665&Itemid=78.

CHAPTER 10

57. L. Srole, T.S. Langner, et al., *Mental Health in the Metropolis, The Midtown Manhattan Study* (New York University Press, July 1978).

58. T.H. Holmes, and R.H. Rahe, The Social Readjustment Rating Scale, *Journal of Psychosomatic Research,* Vol. 11 (1967), pp. 213–218.

59. Swiss Development Cooperation (SDC) report on IDE hand-pump initiative in Vietnam, Berne, 2002.

60. Paul Polak, Deepak Adhikari, Bob Nanes, Dan Salter, and Sudarshan Suryawanshi, "Transforming Rural Water Access Into Profitable Business Opportunities," in "Beyond Domestic: Case Studies on Poverty and Productive Uses of Water at the Household Level," by Patrick Moriarty et al., IRC International Water and Sanitation Centre (Delft, the Netherlands: 2004), pp. 153–172.

CHAPTER 11

61. http://www.oecd.org/document/40/0,2340,en_2649_34447_36418344_1_1_1_1,00.html.

62. http://www.time.com/time/magazine/article/0,9171,923275,00.html.

63. Suresh Kumar, Foreword to *Roadmap for the Emerging Markets* (United Kingdom: Nicholas Hall & Company: November 1, 2003), pp. i–vii.

64. Suresh Kumar, *Benchmarking for OTC* (United Kingdom: Nicholas Hall & Company: July 2005), pp. 169–170.

RESOURCES

Cooper-Hewitt Exhibit Catalog. *Design for the Other 90%*. New York: Cooper-Hewitt National Design Museum, 2007.

Easterly, William. "Was Development Assistance a Mistake?" *The American Economic Review* (May 2007): Vol. 97, No. 2.

www.nyu.edu/fas/institute/dri/Easterly/File/ Was_Development_Assistance_a_Mistake.pdf.

Easterly, William. *The White Man's Burden: Why the West's Efforts to Aid the Rest Have Done So Much Ill and So Little Good.* New York: Penguin Press, 2006.

Heierli, Urs, and Paul Polak. "Poverty Alleviation as a Business. The Market Creation Approach to Development." Swiss Agency for Development and Cooperation (May 2000).

Nagayets, Oksana. "Small Farms: Current Status and Key Trends." Future of Small Farms Research Workshop (International Food Policy Research Institute), Wye College, United Kingdom, June 26–29, 2005.

www.ifpri.org/events/seminars/2005/smallfarms/sfproc/Appendix_InformationBrief .pdf.

Polak, Paul. "The Big Potential of Small Farms." *Scientific American* special issue (September 2005): Crossroads for Planet Earth.

Postel, Sandra. *Pillar of Sand: Can the Irrigation Miracle Last?* New York: W.W. Norton and Co., 1999.

Postel, Sandra, Paul Polak, Fernando Gonzales, and Jack Keller. "Drip Irrigation for Small Farmers: A New Initiative to Alleviate Hunger and Poverty." *Water International* (March 2001): Vol. 26, No. 1.

Schumacher, E.F. *Small Is Beautiful: Economics as if People Mattered.* New York: Harper & Row, 1973.

United Nations Department of Economic and Social Affairs. Millennium Development Goals Report 2006. UN Statistics Division (June 2006).

http://mdgs.un.org/unsd/mdg.

ACKNOWLEDGMENTS

I've spent so much time on the road for the past twenty-five years, it's a wonder that my wife, Aggie, didn't leave me years ago. Instead, she supports my work and we love each other. My daughters, Amy, Kathryn, and Laura, have their own lives now, but when they were teenagers, they played the theme song from *Man of La Mancha* whenever I returned from a trip tired and discouraged. They share my dream for ending poverty, and give me some of my keep-on-going energy.

Writing a book is hard work. I was going to say *very* hard work, but I heard a voice in my head admonishing me to cross out the word *very*. "It weakens what you are trying to say," the voice said. It was my friend Fred Platt, a Denver physician and author, who thoroughly edited every draft of this book, and whose editorial voice has become indelibly embedded in my brain.

Steve Piersanti is a uniquely talented editor, and his suggestions gave shape and focus to the manuscript. The spirited discussions I had with my lifelong friend Arnold Ludwig during long walks along the Rhode Island seashore helped me reformulate and clarify my concepts. Bhimsen Gurung, who worked for twenty years in Nepal's agriculture extension system and plays a major leadership role in IDE Nepal. He joined me in interviews with Krishna Bahadur Thapa and his family, and Mr. Gurung's love of rural people and his good humor brought energy to our conversations. Thanks also go to Mr. Ashok Baral, assistant engineer, IDE Nepal, one of IDE's many remarkable field staff members, who collected detailed information about Bahadur's farm.

Many of the things I have learned about poverty come directly from the commitment and continued learning of IDE's several hundred staff members operating in rural villages. Gerry Dyck was IDE's first field staff member. He was twenty-six and fresh out of college when I met him for the first time in Toronto's Malton airport on the way to Somalia. Gerry had done very well with a summer business that introduced the use of hydraulic lifts to paint grain silos, and now he wanted to do something to make a difference in the world. He had heard from Art DeFehr, a businessman who was a role model for many young people, that I was going to Somalia to do something useful in refugee camps, so Gerry got on the plane on his own nickel. I spent four months with him in Somalia getting the donkey cart project started, and then he took over and did a great job. Now he runs a successful carpet import business in Canada and the United States.

Most of the people who come to work for IDE have a story much like Gerry Dyck's. They see in IDE a vehicle for them to accomplish their dreams. I have described what I learned from Gerry's work in the donkey cart project in several places in this book. Much of what I have written about is derived from programs implemented by hundreds of remarkable IDE staff members over the past twenty-five years. I will mention just a few and let them speak for the rest. Deepak Adhikari is a Nepali engineer who invested his creativity in the design of the Nepal low-cost drip system, as well as in a variety of water-storage devices. Abdus Sobhan got his engineering degree in Dhaka and worked for IDE for fifteen years. He knows more about treadle pumps, and how to design and build and fix them, than anybody I have met. As IDE country director in Bangladesh, Bob Nanes was a major architect of bringing national treadle pump sales from thirty thousand to one hundred twenty-five thousand a year, creating new models for rural marketing. Then Bob managed the Nepal program for twelve years as it introduced innovations such as the village collection centers I describe in *Out of Poverty*, where seventy or so farm families bring their vegetables to be sold by a commissioned sales agent.

Jim and Debbie Taylor and their dedicated staff have accomplished miracles by marketing treadle pumps and affordable irrigation in Myanmar. Amitabha Sadangi has brought hundreds of thousands of small-plot farmers out of poverty with affordable irrigation and access to markets, as well as initiating the IDE program in India, now an autonomous organization. Nguyen Van Quang and his team have created models for the unsubsidized marketing of latrines to poor customers in Vietnam, and Mike Roberts and his team have done the same thing for seven-dollar ceramic water filters in Cambodia. Xaopeng Luo, an economist who was one of the leaders of decollectivization in China and whose family lived through the Mao era, taught me more about Chinese history and culture during our long overnight trips by rail to provinces in the Yellow River Basin than I could have ever learned from a book. Fritz Kramer at the IDE head office is the key leader for the evolution of the PRISM model that plays a catalytic role in the process of connecting farmers with markets. Bob Yoder and Zenia Tata have helped formulate many of the concepts in this book. Board members such as Bill Fast, Al Doerksen, and Art and Frank DeFehr in Canada, Paul Myers, Michael Edesess, and Mohan Uttarwar in the United States, and Michael Lipton and Linda Macleod Brown in the United Kingdom have done much to create and maintain the IDE model described in this book.

Jack Keller is a world authority on irrigation and an IDE board member. Jack brought the IDE low-cost drip-irrigation system to the world market-ready point, working closely with IDE India and J.N. Rai. After defining the world standards for conventional drip irrigation, he recanted and created a new set of standards for small farms. Jack has made affordable small-farm irrigation visible and credible to the world irrigation community. Bob Havener, also an IDE board member and now deceased, brought small-farm agriculture to the agriculture leaders in the world. Michael Lipton has provided critical input on rural poverty. Sandra Postel is a longtime friend who educated me about water and the environment, and Vern Ruttan has always provided invaluable guidance in agriculture economics, along with my Boulder friend Wyn Owen.

In 2005, I met four people who changed forever my thinking about design. I met Michael and Karin Cronan of Cronan Design, Ann Willoughby from Willoughby Design Group, and Cheryl Heller of Heller Communications at the Aspen Design Summit. We went from there to a two-day brainstorming session in Nova Scotia, and the brainstorming has never stopped. It helped create, along with Barbara Bloemink, the Cooper Hewitt exhibit "Design for the Other 90%," and helped me drill down to the essence of what I and IDE have learned over the past 25 years, much of which is distilled in the pages of this book

I have collaborated for many years with Urs Heierli, who provided innovative leadership for IDE's work with small-acreage farmers as the coordinator for Swiss Development Cooperation in Bangladesh and later in India, and we have collaborated on many poverty initiatives and concepts for the past twenty years. SDC provided active donor leadership on the interaction between smallholder irrigation and the environment. Karin Roleofs, from the Dutch foreign ministry, has been an important friend and advisor, and the foreign ministry has provided important support for IDE's work, as has the Lemelson Foundation and my friends Philip and Donna Berber from Glimmer of Hope Foundation. I have great admiration for the Bill and Melinda Gates Foundation, which also supports IDE's work. I like very much its willingness to consider new solutions to old problems and its insistence on measurable impacts and scalability for every viable project.

Most of all, I hope *Out of Poverty* gives voice to thousands of stubborn dollar-a-day farmers like Krishna Bahadur Thapa, his son Deu, and the other members of his family. Their story inspires me, and I hope to pass on some of that inspiration to you.

INDEX

ABOUT THE AUTHOR

"I thought American water wizard Paul Polak was half-mad when I was chasing him around the Zambian countryside as he tried to bring cheap irrigation systems to small farmers," said *National Geographic* writer Fen Montaigne after spending a week with Polak in Zambia.

"But Polak is an admirable character, and it was good fun trailing behind this dynamo. On the Kefue River he brought his road show to an impoverished village. Hundreds of people gathered as Polak demonstrated how a treadle pump—a cheap, foot-operated water pump—could irrigate their fields. As I and younger members of his staff wilted and headed for shade, Polak—drenched in sweat—continued to charge around, persuading villagers that small things like a pump could change their lives."

Montaigne sometimes became pretty bored on this trip as Polak talked to farmer after farmer, learning in meticulous detail how they lived their lives, dreamed their dreams, earned their incomes, and what they thought could bring them out of poverty. This book is based on Polak's extended conversations with more than three thousand small-acreage farmers in developing countries. What he learned from these remarkable, stubborn survival entrepreneurs became the simple operating principles of the organization he founded, International Development Enterprises (IDE), which has helped more than 17 million people who survive on less than a dollar a day to move out of poverty.

Polak has written more than a hundred papers and articles on water, agriculture, design, and development, as well as in the field of mental health. He has been the subject of articles in print media such as *National Geographic, Scientific American, Forbes, Harpers, The New York Times,* and the *Wall Street Journal.* Awards include being named 2003 Entrepreneur of the Year for the Western States by Ernst and Young, the 2004 Tech Museum Prize for design of IDE's low-cost drip-irrigation system, and, also in 2004, the *Scientific American* Top Fifty for his contribution to agricultural policy.

ABOUT IDE

IDE (International Development Enterprises) started twenty-five years ago when three concerned individuals agreed to put up ten thousand dollars each to get it going. Art DeFehr was running Palliser Furniture, a business his dad started which quickly grew into the biggest furniture company in Canada. Don Hedrick ran a supermarket and shopping center in Lancaster, Pennsylvania, and Paul Polak worked as a psychiatrist and in his spare time as an entrepreneur. From its first project, which built and sold five hundred donkey carts to refugee entrepreneurs in Somalia, to its present focus on intensive profitable agriculture on small farms, IDE's mission has been to use practical business strategies to increase the incomes of dollar-a-day poor people.

In the beginning, I worked out of a bedroom in my house as the only staff member, and I worked for the first seven years as a volunteer, living from the money I made as an entrepreneur in other enterprises. Our first grant funds came from the government of Canada and the UN for the donkey cart project, and then we got another grant from the Canadian government to sell treadle pumps in Bangladesh and other countries, a project that turned into a big winner. Even at this early point twenty-two years ago, we sold the treadle pump at a fair market price, and as in the donkey cart project, the poor people who invested got three times their money back in the first year.

IDE has 13 people in its head office in Denver and 550 full-time staff who come from the nine countries where we directly implement our projects—Bangladesh, India, Nepal, Cambodia, Vietnam, Myanmar, Zambia, Zimbabwe, and Ethiopia. IDE has had an impact on the lives of 3.5 million dollar-a-day small-farm families (17.5 million individuals) since its inception, and is working together with its partners to reach 30 million families by 2020.

IDE achieves results in challenging environments of extreme poverty, poor infrastructure, disease, and war. With 90 percent of its employees locally employed in these countries, IDE uses the entrepreneurial approach described in this book to succeed where traditional development models have failed. IDE listens to what its customers, the rural poor, say about their needs and then develops appropriate, affordable solutions that increase their incomes. These solutions include developing and marketing technologies for water access and control, providing expertise and training, and increasing access to markets.

More information is available at www.ide-international.org.

About Berrett-Koehler Publishers

Berrett-Koehler is an independent publisher dedicated to an ambitious mission: Creating a World That Works for All.

We believe that to truly create a better world, action is needed at all levels—individual, organizational, and societal. At the individual level, our publications help people align their lives with their values and with their aspirations for a better world. At the organizational level, our publications promote progressive leadership and management practices, socially responsible approaches to business, and humane and effective organizations. At the societal level, our publications advance social and economic justice, shared prosperity, sustainability, and new solutions to national and global issues.

A major theme of our publications is "Opening Up New Space." They challenge conventional thinking, introduce new ideas, and foster positive change. Their common quest is changing the underlying beliefs, mindsets, and structures that keep generating the same cycles of problems, no matter who our leaders are or what improvement programs we adopt.

We strive to practice what we preach—to operate our publishing company in line with the ideas in our books. At the core of our approach is *stewardship*, which we define as a deep sense of responsibility to administer the company for the benefit of all of our "stakeholder" groups: authors, customers, employees, investors, service providers, and the communities and environment around us.

We are grateful to the thousands of readers, authors, and other friends of the company who consider themselves to be part of the "BK Community." We hope that you, too, will join us in our mission.

A BK CURRENTS BOOK

This book is part of our BK Currents series. BK Currents books advance social and economic justice by exploring the critical intersections between business and society. Offering a unique combination of thoughtful analysis and progressive alternatives, BK Currents books promote positive change at the national and global levels. To find out more, visit www.bkcurrents.com.

Be Connected

VISIT OUR WEBSITE

Go to www.bkconnection.com to read exclusive previews and excerpts of new books, find detailed information on all Berrett-Koehler titles and authors, browse subject-area libraries of books, and get special discounts.

SUBSCRIBE TO OUR FREE E-NEWSLETTER

Be the first to hear about new publications, special discount offers, exclusive articles, news about bestsellers, and more! Get on the list for our free e-newsletter by going to www.bkconnection.com.

GET QUANTITY DISCOUNTS

Berrett-Koehler books are available at quantity discounts for orders of ten or more copies. Please call us toll-free at (800) 929-2929 or e-mail us at bkp.orders@aidcvt.com.

HOST A READING GROUP

For tips on how to form and carry on a book reading group in your workplace or community, see our website at www.bkconnection.com.

JOIN THE BK COMMUNITY

Thousands of readers of our books have become part of the "BK Community" by participating in events featuring our authors, reviewing draft manuscripts of forthcoming books, spreading the word about their favorite books, and supporting our publishing program in other ways. If you would like to join the BK Community, please contact us at bkcommunity@bkpub.com.